HANDBUILT

A Modern Potter's Guide to Handbuilding with Clay

LILLY MAETZIG

photography by India Hobson

quadrille

PROJECTS

INTRODUCTION

When I was little, I would often stay with my grandparents, Leah and Poppa, in New Plymouth, New Zealand, where I am from. Leah always made us porridge for breakfast in the mornings, garnished with brown sugar and a little bit of milk, which formed a moat around the edge of the bowl. We didn't have porridge at home, so it was always a treat when Leah placed my bowl in front of me at the table. She would proudly say that she made porridge for the Queen, and I never really knew if that was a joke or not. It wouldn't surprise me, because her porridge was the best I have ever eaten, to this day.

As Poppa and I sat opposite each other at the table, chatting about whatever and eating porridge fit for royalty, I felt as though we were digging for treasure. Each spoonful was an uncovering, one bite closer. At the bottom of the shallow bowl was the stark blue-and-white icon that I now know as the Willow pattern. I didn't know what it was then, or how iconic that pattern was in and out of the ceramics world, but it was such a treat to see it when finishing breakfast, and every other meal at Leah and Poppa's. I would trace the birds in the sky and the tiny people on the bridge with my spoon, and wonder about who those people were and what the trees looked like in real life.

I don't remember many other ceramics from when I was little, apart from the funny little cups with chickens on them that were at my Nana's house, which I liked because they were so silly. As I sat at that table at Leah and Poppa's, if I looked to my left and a little bit behind me, I could see the whole collection of that Willow-pattern dinner set proudly adorning the china cabinet. Thinking back to this reminds me that there was another china cabinet in the front room at Leah and Poppa's house, but I wasn't really ever interested in what was in there. It was the fact that I was able to eat off the Willow pieces that I found so enticing and special; they weren't hiding away from us but were little art pieces made to be used.

This is my earliest memory of ceramics. It is the moment when I first entered that world, without knowing that years later I would be making functional ceramics for other people to use, maybe for other little kids to eat their porridge from. Since living in London, I have visited the factory in Stoke-on-Trent where the Willow-pattern pieces were produced. It feels very full circle, having moved half a world away and now working in the ceramics industry. Those plates and bowls of my grandparents were left to me when they passed away, a true treasure now.

After leaving high school, where I spent most of my time immersed in the art classrooms, I headed off to art school. I studied (aka snuck off for infinite coffees with my best friend Chloé) for three years and obtained a Bachelor of Design in 2013 with a major in visual arts. It was there,

at art school, where I first touched clay. One of our 3-D design projects was in mould-making, so to learn the basics we looked at plaster moulds and the process of slip casting. I made a whole lot of ceramic milk bottles, using a glass one as the master for the mould. Looking back now, I think this was like jumping in at the deep end of ceramics. Not understanding any of the basics of clay – how it works, how it changes, the infinite ways it can be used – meant that my whole class didn't really know what we were doing but had loads of fun doing it. I was mystified by the way the clay changed after it left our classroom and the technicians had put it through the kilns. When everything came back a week or so later, glazed and much sturdier, I was immediately obsessed.

We didn't do any functional ceramics at art school, so after I graduated I headed to my local pottery club to find out about evening classes. Being fresh out of art school, I wasn't really intending to do functional stuff there either, but more sculptural things. My sister-in-law and I signed up for a two-hour session every fortnight, during which time we could use the space however we liked. There was no proper class plan, but just a teacher hanging out and helping students with whatever they fancied making. As the teacher was a wheel thrower, and there were a few wheels spare, I sat down and gave it a go on the first night.

I was terrible. Yet, however terrible I was, I was also very stubborn; I had to sit there and make something, or I would go home feeling upset and frustrated. I ended up throwing for all of the two-hour sessions of the whole 12-week course, and then signed up for the next course and did the same again.

I was so intent on throwing that I completely ignored handbuilding for that first year. I had thought that I should try some handbuilding at the beginning of my pottery journey, that I should get the basics of clay down before even sitting at a wheel – it would have improved my whole process immensely – but I was laser-focussed on that wheel. I started to understand how to form a cylinder or a bowl, but not really how to treat the clay when it was off the wheel. I wasn't very good at making complex things that had handles or spouts, for example, because clay in this different, non-wheel context didn't make sense to me.

A year later, however, after moving to London, I got myself into a shared studio where I had more time to experiment and make different sorts of pieces. I started playing with handbuilding and, proving my theory right, became a much better potter for it.

I love the way that clay is so tactile and ready to be formed, and I truly believe that the draw to make things from clay with our hands is imprinted in our DNA. It is something that we have known and done for so long – the advent of the vessel to store food and gather water has literally shaped the society we live in today. Moreover, the make-up of clay – silica, alumina and water – is virtually the same as it was thousands of years ago. The cup that we sip our tea from and the beaker that carried our ancestors' grains thousands of years ago is made from the same stuff.

Handmade pottery is an ancient craft. The first known ceramics to be made by humans are estimated to be from 24,000 BC, while the first known vessels were made much more recently in 9,000 BC. The pottery wheel wasn't invented for another few thousand years (around 4000 BC), so the techniques we will be covering in this book really are some of the oldest and most traditional ways to form clay. It is a privilege to be able to work with something that is so steeped in history and tradition.

Clay is a truly magical material. When a piece goes into the kiln as fragile clay and comes out a completely different thing, it seems like alchemy. One of the most satisfying things, for me, is seeing a successful piece come out of the kiln, changed, and much more permanent. It is also a huge privilege for me to be able to share some of what I know with you through this book.

HOW TO USE
THIS BOOK

This book can be used by anybody – those who are brand new to pottery as well as anyone wanting a refresher. If you predominantly use the wheel, it may be a handy tool for you if you want to work with clay in a different way and explore some alternative techniques. It can also be used for inspiration when you aren't sure what to make next and, like a guidebook, it takes you through the various stages of making an object.

Starting by exploring the three main techniques for making ceramics, and later looking at decoration, glazing and firing; the book is split into different parts: Getting Started, Essentials and Projects. You can read it from start to finish or dip in as you wish, using it like an encyclopaedia and flicking to the pages where you need a bit more guidance. You could also start with the Projects and head back to Essentials when you need help with something specific.

Always remember that there is more than one way to make a cup. This is a guidebook to help you become the best potter that you can be. I have explained the way that I do things but it's not always the way I was taught. If you find a different way to do something that works better for you, then of course do that. It's your practice and you should do things in a way that is most efficient and/or enjoyable for you.

GETTING STARTED
The first part of the book helps you to get set up. It has tips on workspace preparation, health and safely, how to choose clay, how to wedge, and all the materials, tools and equipment you might need. If you are a complete beginner, please do read this section before getting started. You may even find it helpful if you have been potting for a while.

ESSENTIALS
This section is designed to show you the very basics, three of the main pillars of handbuilding: pinch, coil and slab building. They can be used individually or all together. I have split them into three basic techniques but they often overlap and share skills.

This section also contains a few extras that are very helpful in handbuilding, such as plaster work, texture work and surface decoration. I have also covered a little bit about adding colour to your work, glazing and firing.

PROJECTS
You can jump straight to the projects if you are here for inspiration. This section includes 22 projects, which have been designed for you to browse through as you would recipes in a cookbook. The projects can be made exactly as shown, or you can use them as a guide to make something similar but in your own style. Some of the projects require templates, these are available to download and print from: www.hardiegrant.com/uk/quadrille/handbuilt

GETTING STARTED

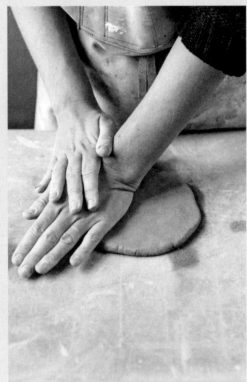

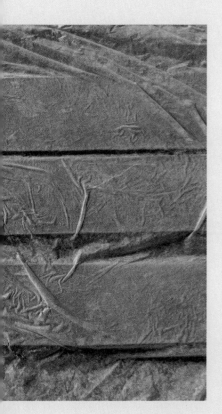

WORKSPACE

Your workspace can be anywhere that works for you, be it a kitchen table or a spacious studio. Wherever you choose, make sure you feel comfortable there to be free with your creativity. Think of it as a sacred space that is yours for being artistic and exploring what you can make with clay. I believe it is important that you don't put too much pressure on yourself to make something perfect, but rather to embrace the process of playing, experimenting and learning. Find a great playlist, make a cup of tea, get some yummy snacks and enjoy this creative time and space.

SURFACE

You need a porous surface to work on. I love working on untreated wood – MDF (medium-density fibreboard) works perfectly. However, if you are working at home and your worktop is made from glass, sealed wood, plastic or anything with a shiny, varnished or textured finish, I suggest sacrificing a wooden chopping board or using some fabric, such as a tea towel or tablecloth, to help make sure your clay doesn't stick to the surface. I also recommend heading to your local hardware store and grabbing some wooden offcuts, ideally nothing too textured, to use as boards to work on. I like to keep all of my tools in cups to the side of my work surface so that everything is easy to grab.

WORKING WITH CLAY

Clay should be tightly wrapped up in its bag when it is not being used, as exposure to the air will start the drying process. There is loads of information on page 18–20 on how to choose the best clay for you. Any clay that has been prepared should also be tightly covered in plastic to prevent it from drying out until you are ready to use it. You can reuse any plastic that you have around – I tend to keep large sheets of plastic that I receive deliveries in for use in the studio; this keeps waste to a minimum and a piece of single-use plastic can be useful for years.

Any clay offcuts that you don't use can be recycled. Start by finding two containers, buckets or tubs into which you can put these offcuts as you are working. One is for wet and mouldable clay. This container should have a lid that seals well, or some plastic that can go over the clay to prevent it from drying out any further; you can occasionally spray it with some water so that it stays nice and soft. The other container is for clay that is leather-hard or dry; this should be left open so that the clay can fully dry out.

In my studio I have large tubs on castors so that I can recycle about a month's worth of clay in one go. Depending on the size of your production, you may choose to use buckets, tubs or smaller containers that can live on a tabletop or shelf. More information about reclaiming clay can be found on page 28–31.

STORAGE

If you are working from home, try to find a suitable place where your pieces can dry out of harm's way. Dry clay is incredibly fragile and well-meaning family members, especially kids or pets, could quite easily break your work if it is stored in a vulnerable spot. A high shelf is a good option for storing your pieces before firing.

WATER

Access to water is important in ceramics. If you have a sink in your studio, you should make sure you have a clay trap installed to catch any clay sediment before it goes through the plumbing system. Clay is heavier than water and will settle in pipes, eventually blocking them. If you aren't able to have a clay trap, a common way of dealing with water in a studio is by employing a three-bucket system. Wash your hands and tools in bucket 1, which will be the dirtiest bucket. Rinse them off in bucket 2 and do a final rinse, if needed, in bucket 3. Leave bucket 1 to settle for a few hours or overnight, then pour the water off down the drain and pour the clay either into the reclaim bucket if it is clean or, if it is contaminated with other bits, into the bin or garden. Bucket 2 then becomes bucket 1, and the empty bucket gets filled with fresh water to continue the cycle. This is a great way to ensure that you take care of your plumbing. Even with a clay trap in my studio, I use this system.

If you find that the clay is drying out quickly as you are working on a piece, you will notice the surface may crack slightly, particularly on rims. You can dip your finger in some water and lightly wet the surface. A drop of water goes a long way – you don't want to get the clay too wet but just bring it back to the point before it starts to crack. If you don't wet the clay it will continue to dry out and may form deeper cracks that compromise the structure of the pot.

WORKSPACE SAFETY

Working with clay is a reasonably safe practice, however there are a few things around your workspace that can keep you as safe and healthy as possible.

One of the main issues in ceramics is airborne silica finding its way into your lungs. Clay contains a lot of silica, and when the clay dries the silica particles can become airborne, which can then be inhaled. To keep dust to a minimum, you should always have a large bowl or bucket of water and a sponge or cloth nearby so you can periodically tidy and wipe down your workspace. It is very easy to sponge down your surfaces as you work to prevent dust from building up. You should also avoid dry sweeping or vacuuming in your studio space; it is better to mop the floor so that any dust that has settled there doesn't become airborne. Household vacuum cleaners generally don't have filters fine enough for silica dust – ideally your studio will have hard floors, rather than carpet or rugs, which will hold on to the silica dust.

If you have a kiln, it is important to have it wired in by a certified electrician. It should be placed on a concrete or tile floor, not wood or carpet, and it needs to be a minimum of 30cm (12in) away from any walls. Kilns get extremely hot during firing, so make sure there is no paper or any other flammable material under, around or on top of the kiln when it is on. Ensure visitors to your studio, especially kids and pets, stay away from the kiln while it is on or cooling, to avoid burns.

Glaze materials can sometimes seem a little intimidating or scary if you aren't sure what they are. In a nutshell, glazes are made from fine particles of silica and different types of rocks. However, there are a few toxic and dangerous chemicals that were once commonplace in ceramics but aren't really used any more, such as lead and, amazingly, uranium. These toxic materials are quite difficult to purchase now – if you are purchasing a commercial glaze, for example, it will be clear if it is for decorative use only or safe to use on functional pieces. If you are making a glaze from scratch, however, you should always look into the ingredients to make sure you are not inadvertently using something harmful. No matter what the material, you should always use a dust mask rated for silica use when dealing with dry materials to avoid breathing them in. Learn more about this in the glaze section on page 74.

From the top: wet clay, dry clay, bisqueware and glazed

CLAY

Clay, what a material! I believe there is something in us humans that has a deep connection to clay. It is essentially mud, a special mud that changes so dramatically in the kiln that its chemical composition is altered, which feels a little bit like alchemy when you unload the kiln. The most common clays for pottery are earthenware, stoneware and porcelain. They all have different qualities and features, such as firing temperature, colour, durability and texture, which may help you to pick the best one for your project.

All clay is made up of alumina, silica and water. It sometimes contains other things, such as iron and sand, which don't really have anything to do with the chemical make-up of the clay itself. Clay particles are flat, disc-like platelets, which stack up on each other to become very strong. This makes it such a special material as it enables it to exist in completely opposite states: wet clay is plastic, meaning it can be moulded and shaped; dry clay is hard but brittle; fired ceramic is very tough and durable.

While it is in the kiln, clay goes through a chemical change to become ceramic. It is an important change, as the high temperatures remove the chemically bound water, and the remaining alumina and silica become much more tightly bound. This makes for ceramic ware that is either water resistant or waterproof (vitrified). The removal of that water also means that the pieces will shrink a lot, sometimes up to 15 per cent.

GREENWARE

There are important stages that clay goes through to become ceramic. Greenware is the term used to describe all the different stages of clay before it goes into the kiln.

WET CLAY

This is clay with a high water content. It is very plastic, mouldable and squishy. It can be made into almost anything at this stage, although there is a limit to what you can do with wet clay, as many designs need the clay to firm up a little so that it can hold its shape without deforming.

LEATHER HARD

The clay has dried a little but it is still the same colour as wet clay. You can make a mark on it easily – for example, you could scratch it with the back of your fingernail – but it is rigid. This is a very important moment for the clay, as you can join, slowly shape, smooth, texture or paint it. It can also be dampened down with a sponge and become mouldable again (up to a limit). This is the point at which handles are usually attached and most pieces are finished. You need to wrap the clay in plastic to keep it at this leather-hard stage – in which it can remain for a long time if it properly wrapped.

BONE DRY

Dry clay is hard but very brittle. You will notice that its colour has changed, becoming a little lighter, and it has shrunk slightly, as much of the water has evaporated. It is important to handle dried pieces with care – don't pick cups up by the handle or lift anything by the rim as the clay can very easily snap and it is difficult to reattach broken pieces at this stage.

All forms of greenware can be recycled, so if you have any offcuts or pieces that you don't want to fire, you can add all of them to the reclaim bucket (see page 28).

BISQUEWARE

You can bisque fire your clay after it has been shaped and refined, and has had the chance to fully dry. A bisque firing is when you fire your pieces to around 1,000°C (1,882°F). They will change in the kiln, going from clay to ceramic. The bisqueware will be very porous, like a sponge. This is the stage that you will glaze your pieces, and after glazing, they go back into the kiln. You can learn all about the firing process in the Firing section on pages 80–84.

If you put clay into the kiln wet, it will explode. The water trapped inside of the clay will swiftly turn into steam and the pressure build up will cause some pretty catastrophic damage to wet pieces, and often pieces nearby in the kiln.

After the piece has been bisque fired, it can be glazed. It goes back into the kiln one last time, and the glaze will melt and fuse to the ware. The ceramic goes through one last change, and any remaining water, chemical or physical, will be fired out. The piece shrinks a little bit more, and all of the particles fuse closer together still, making stoneware vitrified and glazed earthenware water resistant. Learn more about the different types of clays and all of their properties on pages 18–20, and learn more about glazing on pages 69–79.

The piece is finished now, unless you would like to apply an overglaze to it. This is a special type of paint, gold or pearl lustre, or ceramic decal that can be applied to the piece. It goes back into the kiln for a third time and is fired up to around 750°C (1,382°F), a low temperature in ceramics, to fuse the overglaze to the piece.

DIFFERENT TYPES OF CLAY

There are three main types of clay that are suitable for the projects in this book: earthenware, stoneware and porcelain. Throughout the book I will use terracotta, which is a type of earthenware, and stoneware.

Deciding on what clay you would like to use is more than just what you like the look of. You need to consider the following: durability and strength; the temperature you would like to fire at; whether your pieces are sculptural or functional. These considerations, along with the finished look of the ceramic itself, will be how you decide. I will go into the pros and cons of each below to guide you in that choice.

EARTHENWARE

This is a low-fire, very commonly, red clay. Terracotta plant pots and red ware are earthenware. It fires somewhere between 1,000°C (1,882°F) and 1,200°C (2,192°F) – any hotter than this and the clay may start to bloat and melt. Earthenware is always porous, even after its final firing, although glazes can be applied to it that make it pretty water-resistant.

Earthenware is a very energy-efficient clay. It costs less to fire than stonewares and porcelains, as earthenware doesn't need to go to such high temperatures. It is the most common type of clay, which makes it cheaper to purchase. You can get amazing colours of earthenware, depending on the amount of iron found in it – usually rich reds and browns, but you can also find white earthenware. Very bright slips and glazes can be use with it, as the oxides don't burn out at the temperatures earthenware is fired to. A great thing about terracotta is that sometimes you would only fire it once, and wouldn't glaze it. Plant pots, for example, are porous and will help to avoid things like root rot by not allowing water to be trapped inside the pot. Cutting out a whole firing, let alone a high temperature firing, makes for much cheaper kiln costs than other types of clay.

This type of clay can, however, be brittle and a lot less durable for functional ware due to it not being fully watertight. It will always take on some amount of water, and sometimes you can find mould or other bacteria growing in the clay or under the glaze. It is less resistant to being used daily in the kitchen or in the dishwasher because of this. If you have an earthenware vase, it is advisable to place a coaster under it so that any moisture that finds its way through the ceramic does not damage the surface it is sitting on.

STONEWARE

With a higher firing point than earthenware, stoneware clay is fired to maturity somewhere between 1,200°C (2,192°F) and 1,300°C (2,372°F), where it will become vitrified (watertight). Glaze can also be applied to stoneware but different recipes will be used (see page 69–79 for more on glazing). Stoneware is my pick for functional ware for the reasons that earthenware isn't: it is strong and durable and with proper care, it can last for thousands of years. It's overwhelming to think that something we can create can exist for that long. It can be used with foods and liquids and will withstand the dishwasher. A properly fired stoneware vessel will not leak in the way that earthenware would. It does cost more to buy and to fire it, however, as it needs to go in the kiln at much higher temperatures.

Stonewares are often a creamy buff to white in colour and it is harder to get the lovely rich reds of earthenware pieces, although it is possible. It is also more difficult to achieve bright colours as surface decoration at stoneware temperatures, so ceramicists may find they are spending more money on specific colourants and oxides to achieve this.

PORCELAIN

A very pure form of clay, porcelain is high fire, ranging from 1,250°C to 1,350°C (2,282°F to 2,462°F). It is known for its stark white colour, as it is not muddied with iron-rich minerals like earthenware and stoneware usually are, although colours can be added to it. Glazes look beautiful on porcelain, as it is such a pure white canvas to work on.

Porcelain makes for incredibly beautiful pieces when fired. However, it is very difficult to work with – cracks and warping are more common with porcelain than other clays, but the reward of a well-made piece really pays off when unloading the kiln. If used thinly enough, porcelain can be translucent when fired, which makes it an ideal clay to use for decorative objects such as lampshades and sculptures. It is also great for functional ware as it is very tough and durable, but it is very expensive, both to buy and to fire.

OTHER STUFF TO NOTE

CLAY HAS A MEMORY

That sounds a little woo-woo, I know. Clay particles are disc-like platelets that arrange very neatly on top of each other – stacking like bricks, in fact – giving clay its plasticity. However, these particles are rearranged, just slightly, every time you move and handle the clay, and this can lead to weird warping issues when the clay goes through the kiln. When working with wet clay, ensure that you aren't too rough with it. That means, when picking up a slab that will become a plate, for example, don't let it flop around, but try to keep it as flat as possible at all times. Generally, be gentle with the clay when it is wet – if not, it inevitably leads to the piece developing cracks or warping. Treat it with love and care and, scientifically, your clay will, remember, that.

GROG

Whichever clay you pick, I would recommend using a grogged version for handbuilding, if possible. Grog is a kind of sand that has been added to the clay. It makes the pieces shrink a little less and makes handbuilt pieces more resistant to cracking and warping. It does have some texture, though, so if you are looking for a super-smooth finish it may not be the answer.

OTHER TYPES OF CLAY

Here is a quick run down of some other types of clay, although these aren't recommended for the projects in this book.

AIR-DRYING CLAY

While you could use air-drying clay for some of the projects in this book, this type of clay doesn't go in the kiln so it will never become watertight. That means that even if you paint and seal it, it will always break down in water. Do take note of that if you decide to use it for your work. Air-drying clay is a good choice for jewellery and ornamental pieces, however.

SLIP-CASTING CLAY

A technique where liquid clay is poured into plaster moulds is known as slip casting. Slip is a liquid with additives that keep the clay suspended in the water – it is just the same as earthenware, stoneware or porcelain, but in liquid form.

It is often used in industrial ceramics as it is a very efficient way to make multiples of the same item. It also means that you can create reasonably intricate designs from the moulds, so is popular in both functional and sculptural ware.

BALL CLAY

Sold in powered form and usually mixed with other ceramic materials, ball clay is used mostly in industrial settings and very rarely in pottery. Items such as tiles, bathroom sinks and toilets are made from ball clay. It is also an ingredient in bricks and porcelain insulators in the electrical industry, among other things. Ball clay is very strong and plastic, but shrinks massively.

FIRE CLAY

Also usually sold in powder form, fire clay has a much higher firing temperature (1,600°C/2,912°F) than all of the above clays, which makes it very heat-resistant. It is used to make items such as kiln and oven bricks, and as an additive to things such as kiln shelves and pizza stones. It is a refractory clay, meaning that it does not deform under intense heat.

SHRINKAGE

It is very helpful to perform a shrink test for your clay body, so that you know how much to expect your clay to move.

1. Roll out a small slab of clay to 10cm.

2. Draw a little ruler onto your clay – mark each centimetre up to 10cm.

3. Fire the clay to the temperature you usually fire to.

4. Compare your new ceramic ruler to your regular ruler and see how much it has moved. If you find that your ceramic ruler measures 9cm (3½in) on your regular ruler, you can see that it has shrunk by 1cm (½in) or 10 per cent.

You can now add 10 per cent to your pieces to get a final size. Working backwards like this is very helpful when you are making items to a specific size – for example, when you are making a candlestick (see pages 143 and 146), you need to know what size to make the hole that will hold the candle, as if it is too big or too small the candle won't fit.

From left to right: greenware, bisqueware and stoneware fired clay rulers

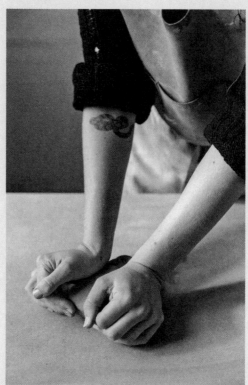

▲ STEP 3.1

▲ STEP 4

WEDGING

Wedging is an important process in pottery. It is an action similar to kneading dough in baking, used to homogenize the clay and to remove any air bubbles. Trapped air in the clay can cause small cracks or blisters on the surface, and badly wedged clay is weak.

The point of wedging is essentially to stack all of the clay particles on top of each other. Clay particles are platelet shaped and, when properly wedged, they line up together and make a very strong bond when fired. I might get in trouble for writing this, but if you are cutting clay straight from the block, out of the bag, you can usually get away with not wedging it. If you cut the clay from the bag and notice that there are air pockets or an inconsistency in moisture, or if you are using saved or reclaimed clay, it will need to be wedged before use.

The three most common ways of wedging are ram's head, spiral, and cut and slam wire wedging (I call this last one 'slam' wedging as sounds more fun). All of these techniques should be performed on a dry, porous surface, such as dry canvas, plaster or unsealed wood. If you are working on a material that is wet or sealed, the clay will very likely get too stuck to the surface. Canvas and wood are great for wedging on when clay is at the ideal level of moisture, whereas plaster is a better choice when the clay is slightly too wet.

RAM'S HEAD

Ram's head wedging is the most common technique for beginner potters to learn. It is very effective for small (200g–1kg/7oz–2¼lb) amounts of clay. It is named ram's head because of the shape it makes.

1. If you are weighing the clay, weigh it out now.

2. With both hands on the clay, pull it up on its edge with your fingers.

3. Push the clay down and away from yourself with the heels of your hands, with even pressure going through both palms. The clay should start to look like a ram's head during this process.

4. Repeat steps 2–3 around 20–50 times, until you can cut the piece of clay in half with a wire without spotting any air bubbles. Pat it into a general ball shape.

Tips

*   Use both your body weight and your arm strength to wedge.

*   Once you are into the swing of wedging, you will feel that it is a fluid, rocking motion.

*   Make sure your hands are pressing down and, at the same time, in towards each other, to ensure the clay isn't just rolling into a flat shape. Concentrate on pressing in rather than down.

- It is important not to fold the clay, as this will create potential for bubbles (and you are trying to press the clay into itself to remove air).

SPIRAL

This is my preferred wedging method. Spiral wedging is great for wedging both small pieces (200g/7oz) up to quite large pieces (2–5kg/4½–11lb) if you have the upper-body strength.

1. If you are weighing the clay, weigh it out now. Pat the clay into a general ball shape. With both hands on the clay, pull it up on its edge with your fingers.

2. Press the clay down and away from you with the heel of your dominant hand. Your non-dominant hand helps by applying pressure, as well as making sure the clay doesn't spread too wide, but the hard work is done with your dominant hand.

3. Bring the clay up onto its edge, turn it 10–15 degrees and repeat step 2. If you are right-handed, turn the clay anticlockwise; if you are left-handed, turn it clockwise.

4. Repeat steps 2–3 around 20–50 times, until you can cut the piece of clay in half with a wire without spotting any air bubbles.

Tips

- This technique may not feel natural to begin with, but once you are used to the flow of movements it requires a lot less concentration than ram's head wedging.

- Like ram's head wedging, spiral wedging is a very fluid, rocking motion.

- Much like ram's head, this is named spiral wedging for the shape it makes - it looks like a bit like a shell when done correctly.

SLAM

Slam wedging is great for wedging clay that has just been reclaimed, or if you want to blend two clays together. Blending clays together is a good solution when you have some very hard clay and some very soft clay, or if you want to create a new colour of clay by mixing two types together. This technique effectively makes thousands of layers of clay very quickly, forcing the air out of the sides of each layer. It uses gravity to help wedge, rather than your upper body doing all of the work.

1. Take approximately 2–5kg (4½–11lb) of clay and cut it in half. The pieces don't need to be equal in weight but they should be around the same width. Slam one of the pieces on top of the other.

2. Turn the clay up on its side, so that the line where the clays have joined is vertical. Using a wire, cut horizontally through the clay.

3. Turn one half of the clay 90 degrees so that the join line is now horizontal.

4. Turn the other half 90 degrees as well, and slam it onto the other piece of clay. All of the join lines should be stacked horizontally.

5. Repeat steps 2–4 around 20–50 times, until the clay seems homogenized and you can't differentiate between each layer.

The beauty of slam wedging is that you are doubling the layers every time you cut and slam. This means that the layers are growing exponentially, so blending two clays together using this method is much quicker, more efficient and a lot less effort than by ram's head or spiral wedging. It is also a very effective way of getting rid of any pent-up stress or anger – just slam it right out on the table and it's gone!

I like to finish off my slam wedging with a quick spiral wedge to tidy up the edges. The clay can then be used straight away or bagged up for use later.

RECLAIM

Something I try to keep in mind is that in a world where there are already so many things, we as makers have some responsibility to be mindful of what else we add. One of the most beautiful things about clay is that if you don't fire a piece, you can return it to its original state over and over again. You can also recycle all of your clay scraps and offcuts, making it a very efficient and environmentally friendly material. I try to be very selective about what I do decide to put in the kiln – if a piece has a flaw or if there is something about it that I don't really like in the first stage, I thank it for what it has taught me and put it into the reclaim bucket to become something else in the future. That way, you can practice and concentrate on getting the form exactly how you would like it and you don't need to waste any more time or resources trying to fix it later.

Reclaiming clay is a very simple process. Water is added to dry clay, starting a process called slaking. This is when the clay particles loosen and become separated from the larger piece they were once part of. It is almost like the clay is melting into the water. Once the clay has slaked down into a clay slop, it can then be placed onto a porous surface, such as a plaster bat. To learn how to make a plaster bats see page 62. The plaster will absorb the excess water, leaving the clay on top ready to wedge. Once the clay has been wedged up, it is ready to be used again.

A good studio setup can make this task a lot less daunting, so make sure you check out the section on preparing your workspace (see page 14–15) before you get started.

▼ STEP 1

▼ STEP 1.1

▲ STEP 3

▲ STEP 4

RECLAIM PROCESS

1. Fill up your bucket with clay scraps and leave everything to dry out. Add water to the scraps – it can be clay water or water straight from the tap. Fully submerge the clay but don't add too much extra after that.

2. Leave the clay to soak and slake down for a minimum of 12 hours – I like to leave mine for at least a week. This ensures proper slaking can occur, as well as ageing the clay a little.

3. Mix the clay with your hands in the bucket for a few minutes. You will either love or hate doing this, there really is no in between. Transfer the clay to plaster bats to dry. (Learn how to make your own plaster bat on page 62.)

4. Spread the clay evenly on your plaster bat(s), 5cm (2in) thick at the most and poke holes into the clay with your fingers to allow the air to dry it more evenly.

5. Once the clay has dried enough that you can peel it off the plaster bat, roll it up into a cylinder. The clay is now ready to be wedged up. Slam wedging is the best method for reclaimed clay (see page 26). Alternatively, it can be stored in a lidded bucket or tightly wrapped in plastic until you are ready to wedge it.

6. Once clay has been through the kiln and fired past about 500°C, it will not be possible to reclaim it. Learn more about the chemical changes that clay goes through in the kiln on page 80.

Tip

If you feel overwhelmed by the reclaim process, it may help to do it in smaller batches, more frequently. I leave a few months of reclaim to do all at once, which can feel like a daunting task. It is much easier to wedge one ball of clay than 10, so do whatever works for you.

Note

Clay contains organic materials, and when they start to break down they can start getting a little stinky. It's completely normal for reclaim to smell a little bit boggy, or to grow mildew on top. You can mix the mildew in, it won't have any effect. If the smell really offends you, try adding a 1–2 tablespoons of white vinegar to the water you add to offset it a little. Adding too much vinegar can impact the plasticity of the clay, so use it sparingly.

TOOLS AND MATERIALS

There are an almost infinite variety of tools that can be used for handbuilding pottery. If you check out any pottery supplies store, you will find an endless number of tools that you can buy for all sorts of niche uses. You can also make do with whatever you have around your house, resulting in a similar outcome, rather than going out and purchasing loads of new things, some of which you may find you will never use.

ESSENTIAL TOOLS

All the tools listed below are must-haves in my practice:

- Bowls of different sizes for water and slip.

- Buckets: some with lids, some without.

- Guides – these are used in slab building to maintain a uniform thickness when rolling the clay out. I recommend heading to your local hardware store to purchase a few flat pieces of wood – I go for about 5–8mm ($\frac{1}{4}$–$\frac{3}{8}$in) thickness. Alternatively, you can usually get guides from your pottery supplies store.

- Potters knife or scalpel.

- Metal and metal kidneys – used for smoothing the clay (also referred to as ribs).

- Pin tool – used to cut the clay, as well as scoring the clay to join. You can make your own by using nylon fishing line and a couple of buttons.

- Serrated metal kidney – used for scoring the clay; it also doubles as a very helpful tool in smoothing clay down.

- Set of scales for weighing the clay.

- Sponges.

- Various wooden boards to work on, the flatter the better.

- Wire – to cut the clay from the block. (You can make your own by using nylon fishing line and a couple of buttons.)

- Wooden knife tool – very useful for blending joins; they are usually double-sided for different types of blending work.

- Wooden rolling pin.

ADDITIONAL TOOLS

All the tools listed below are very handy, but not strictly necessary.

- Banding wheel or cake turner – these can be purchased online, and you'll find a whole world of banding wheels at a fraction of the price.

- General stationery – namely a ruler, paper, pens, pencils, masking tape, scissors.

- Loop tool – used to make handles and coils efficiently, as well as to carve texture into the surface.

- Paintbrushes.

- Shredder/rasp – an incredible tool to shape and carve the clay at the leather-hard stage.

- Sieves – a regular kitchen sieve as well as a finer mesh one (around 100 mesh) for mixing glaze.

MATERIALS

CLAY

Choose between earthenware, stoneware or porcelain for your making. Learn all the differences in the Clay section (see page 17–23). I recommend grogged stoneware for functional ware.

SLIPS, OXIDES AND UNDERGLAZES

These are optional, for if you would like to add colour to your clay. You can purchase small amounts first to have a go with. Read about all the differences in the section on colouring clay (see page 64–67).

GLAZE MATERIALS

I have included a small glaze section here, but glazing could be an entire book on its own as there is a lot to learn. There are many different ingredients and infinite ways to mix them together, so it is hard to narrow down a list of essentials as each ingredient does something quite unique.

I suggest purchasing a couple of commercial glazes from your local pottery supplier before undergoing glaze making, especially if you are early on in your pottery journey.

Two very handy glazes to start with are a good transparent/clear glaze and a good white glaze. You can easily add colourants to these basic glazes for a bit of variation. You can also search your pottery supplier's website to see if there are any special glazes that you like the look of. Once you have done a few test firings, you can look into making your own glazes if you feel drawn to do so.

Make sure the glazes you buy are rated to the temperature your clay fires to – so if you are using stoneware clay, ensure you have stoneware glaze, and if you are working with earthenware clay, use earthenware glaze. You'll encounter all sorts of problems if you have the incorrect glaze, like crazing, crawling or shivering. (See pages 69–79 for an in-depth look at glaze issues.)

ESSENTIALS

MAKING

In this section, we will cover all of the basics that you need to know for actually making your pieces. We will start by making a pot using each of the three main handbuilding techniques: pinch, coil and slab. We will then go through a few other techniques – for example, how to make and use moulds in your work to create consistency in shapes, and how to use and utilize plaster as a clay companion in the studio. We will then look at how to decorate your pieces with texture, underglazes and slips. After all of that, we will look into glazing, the other half of ceramics. Finally, I will show you how to fire your pieces, the differences in kilns and firing, and what to expect when you load and unload a kiln.

PINCH, COIL AND SLAB

These three techniques are the main building blocks of handbuilding, and on the following pages we will learn how to make pots using each method. (The image opposite displays the three techniques from left to right: pinch, coil and slab.) You'll notice that each pot will look different in the end; each method has different uses and outcomes. This will give you a foundational understanding of how and why each technique works, and you can use it as a reference later in the Projects section (see page 86).

PINCH

Pinching is a very basic and lovely way to make a pot. These pots can be used as starters for other larger vessels, but equally they are beautiful in their own right.

A trick when making pinch pots is to only use the amount of clay that you can hold in your hand. Ball the clay up and hold it in the palm of one hand, then cover the clay with your other hand. If you are unable to cover the clay completely with your top hand, you have a little too much; this will make the piece much harder to handle as it grows with your pinching, and can lead to a weak pot. Remove some clay before starting – you can always add a little bit more to the top of the pot later.

Materials and tools

Clay, approx. 150–250g
  (5½–9oz)
Potters knife or scalpel tool
Sponge and water
Optional: serrated and
  smooth metal kidney

Note

Pinch pots are very tangible and show the human element of how they were made. I think this one is especially lovely because of my fingerprints on it, which give it movement and a bit of a soul. If you want a very smooth pot, however, wait for the clay to harden up a bit. When it is leather hard, you can smooth the shape out with a kidney tool.

1. Get some clay out of the bag. You don't want too much, so make sure you can hold it in both hands (see above). As a rough guide, a piece that is between the size of a golf ball and a tennis ball, around 150–250g (5½–9oz); is a good size to aim for.

2. Pat the clay into a ball. If it is straight from the bag, you shouldn't need to do anything to it; if it isn't, you might need to wedge it (see page 25–26). With your dominant hand, make a hole in the clay with your thumb. Have the clay sit on your thumb like a little mushroom and leave about 1cm (½in) of clay between your finger and your thumb.

3. Using a pincer-type of motion, slowly pinch the clay evenly, starting at the bottom of the pot moving slowly around and up, towards the rim. Your pinching motion will move the clay outwards and upwards. After each pinch, rotate the pot ready for the next pinch. Cup the pot with your non-dominant hand, supporting the shape as it grows.

4. Continue pinching the pot, always pinching and rotating all around the pot, base to rim. Once you have pinched around twice, and reached the top of the rim, slowly run your fingers around the pot, feeling for areas that are thicker. Pinch these so that the whole pot is of an even thickness.

▲ STEP 3

▲ STEP 4

5. Continue going over the pot from base to rim a few times until it is a uniform thickness that you are happy with, going no thinner than about 3mm (⅛in).

6. If you would like your rim to be a little more solid, you can gently run a finger or a thumb across it to compress it.

7. If you want your pot to have a flat base, use your work surface to achieve that by gently tapping the clay a few times onto the flat surface.

Tips

•   If you would like the rim to be more even, take your potters knife and very carefully insert at the lowest point of the rim. Very slowly and gently pull the knife through the clay to get a flat rim all the way around, supporting the rim on either side with your other hand.

•   If you find that your pinch pot turns into a bowl when you are trying to make a cup, you need to adjust the angle of your pinching hand. As you are pinching, take note of the shape that the clay is forming. If it is turning into a bowl, change the angle of your wrist so that the clay is being pinched inwards, rather than outwards. The clay will naturally flare outwards, and you need to work against this a little bit to get a cup. It may feel very unnatural, however if your hand is angled too far away from the base of the cup, it will naturally make a very wide shape.

•   Learn how to add a foot ring to the base of your pot by following the instructions on page 94.

▲ STEP 7

ESSENTIALS

SCORING AND SLIPPING

This is how to join two pieces of clay together. It is how you will always treat joins, be it a handle to a cup, a wall to a base, a spout to a teapot or anything else. Scoring both sides of the join helps the pieces of clay grab and hold onto each other. Think of scoring the clay as working on a similar principle to Velcro – the rough areas hold onto each other to create a strong bond.

Slip is clay with water added to it so it becomes a liquid. The slip acts as a glue. When the clay is pressed firmly into place, it will hold itself there and make a strong join as it dries. The aim is for the clay to homogenize and become one piece, so the joins need to be firmly pressed together to make this happen. I like to join when the clay is leather hard so that it can support itself, but this isn't always possible. When joining clay, you should attempt to make sure both pieces of clay are the same level of dryness so that they will shrink at the same rate.

1. Create some slip by placing some clay into a small bowl or dish, and pouring the same amount of water on top of it. With a paintbrush, mix these two together so that you have a slurry of clay. I use a jar of slip that I have had for years, and I add a little handful of clay scraps and water to the jar at the each time I use it.

2. Score both sides of the join with the serrated rib or a pin tool. Apply slip to one of these scored areas.

3. Firmly press the two pieces together, and allow the excess slip squish out the sides of the joins.

4. Use a wooden knife tool to tidy it all up and to blend the squished out slip into the joins.

If you are joining two pieces of very soft clay together, you may need to support the piece – for example, a handle may sag if it is too soft. You can use some extra clay to press into a ball the exact size that you need the support to be.

▲ STEP 2.1

▼ STEP 1

▼ STEP 2

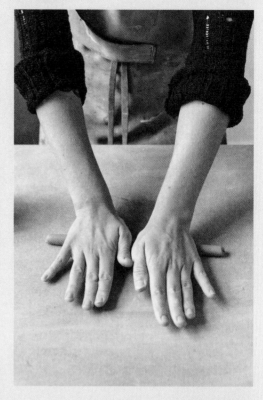

▲ STEP 3

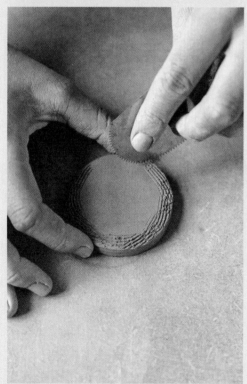

▲ STEP 3.1

COIL

With this method, coil pots are made by layering and joining coils of clay on top of each other, slowly building up a wall. It is a very effective way to make both small and large pots. One of the things I really like about coil pots is that you can choose to either disguise the coils by blending them together or leave them visible on the surface of the pot. I think it is quite romantic to make a decorative feature of the construction and let the coils show the history of how the pot was made.

To make a coil pot, you will need a handful of clay. I generally don't measure the clay for a coil pot, but just grab it from the bag as I go. As a guide, to build a small pot you will need about 250g (9oz) of clay, or you can make a large pot by scaling this up. I will show you how to make a small pot, but the principles apply to larger ones, too. I like to work on a board so that I don't damage the pot by continually picking it up. It is also very helpful to have a banding wheel.

Materials and tools

Clay, approx. 200–300g (7–10½oz)
Scalpel or cookie cutter
Scoring tool or pin tool
Slip
Serrated metal kidney
Flat metal kidney
Sponge

1. Take a handful of clay, and roll or squash a flat base. You don't need to measure this, but it needs to be wide enough for the base of a cup, and around 8mm (⅜in) thick. You can cut a specific shape out with your scalpel or a cookie cutter, or go for a more organic base by freehanding it.

2. Roll your first coil. Take another handful of clay and squash it into a little worm shape. Then, with a steady movement, using your whole hand from the base of your palm all the way to your outstretched fingertips, roll it along the work surface away from you. If you press a bit too hard, you might find that the coil starts to go square. If that happens, you can pause, squash it back down and continue rolling.

3. Using a pin tool or a serrated metal kidney, score the top of the base around the edge where the wall will go. Don't be tentative about it, although don't go so deep that you cut through the clay. Next, apply some slip to the area where you have just scored (see page 43).

4. Place the coil around the edge of the base, pinching off any excess, and press it down firmly.

5. Blend the inside join – you can use the back of a wooden knife tool or with your thumb. The more coil pots you make, the more you'll begin to favour certain tools for certain jobs. Experiment with different tools to see what suits you best.

6. Make more coils. I like to roll loads at once so I don't have to pause in the construction. If it is warm in your house or studio, make sure you cover the coils with some plastic so they don't dry out.

7. Now you are going to add to the pot row by row. Pinch each coil onto the top of the previous coil to join them. You can either make a really long coil and wind it all the way up, or you can go layer by layer. I prefer working with layers, although you should try both to see which you prefer. As your pot grows, you need to be aware of its form – if you want the pot to flare outwards, you need to 'staircase' the coils upwards in that direction; if you want it to come in, stagger the layers inwards in the same way. For more info on this, see the Coil Vase on page 170.

Note

If you have decided to leave the surface of your coil pot with the coils unblended, it is important that you check for any gaps, as this will mean a leaky pot once fired. Do this by bringing your face to the pot's level and, moving it around on the board or banding wheel, check for any light through the wall. If you see any gaps, make sure you press these coils tightly together or plug the holes with a tiny bit of extra clay.

The reason we don't need to score and slip each layer of a coil pot is because each coil is blended into the next. However, if you want to keep the coils visible on the surface of the finished pot, you will need to make sure that each layer is firmly pressed down on the previous one and, if the layers are feeling too dry, add a little drop of water between each one. It is important to press each layer down firmly and pinch it into the coil below to join them.

SMOOTHING THE LAYERS

If you would like a smooth surface, you need to blend each coil onto the next. Generally, I do this in batches of around five layers to save time. Always support the inside of your pot with your opposing hand as you are working on the outside, and vice versa. This will ensure that your pot will not flex and break. Note that if you decide to smooth your whole pot, you must ensure that you can fit your hand into the opening at the top. If you plan on making a form that comes in to a narrow opening, smooth the coils at the base of the pot while it is still wide enough to support.

8. As I am coiling, I blend the coils by pinching the clay into the layer below. You can either do it this way, by pinching it down, or you can bring the clay up from the coil below, whichever you prefer. I do this with my thumb, but it can be done with a wooden knife tool.

9. Once all of your coils are blended, you can choose to clean the surface of the pot up. Using a serrated metal kidney, drag the spikes all over the pot, criss crossing over the whole piece. This will feel counter-intuitive, but it helps very much. If you can, continue supporting the pot on the opposite side as you are working.

10. Using a smooth metal kidney, repeat step 9, but this time you are smoothing all of the marks made by the serrated metal kidney. You may find that the clay needs to harden up a tiny bit if you have just made the pot, so set it aside for a little while until the clay is not squishing under your touch. Equally, if the clay is too hard at this stage, spray it with your water bottle to soften it a little bit.

11. Use a lightly dampened sponge to refine the whole piece and to smooth out any last marks from the kidneys.

12. Allow the pot to dry slowly by draping some plastic over top. This will help to avoid any cracks forming.

▼ STEP 4

▼ STEP 4.1

▲ STEP 5

▲ STEP 8

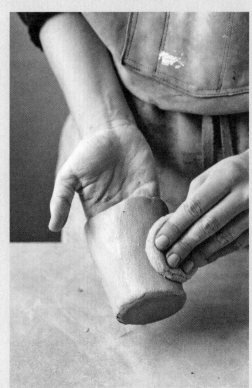

▲ STEP 10

▲ STEP 11

Tips

- If you are having trouble with the shape of your coils, you may be pressing a little too hard as you roll them out. If you are, the coils will start going slightly square, so try to apply a little less pressure.

- If you find your coils are uneven and get too thin in some places and are thicker in others, you need to move your hands along the clay as you are rolling, rather than applying too much pressure on one spot.

- Use two hands for larger coils and start in the middle, moving your hands away from each other as you roll. This will make the coil grow.

- If your coils get too dry as you are rolling them, spray the work surface with water. This will allow the coil to absorb some of the water without getting too wet – otherwise you can end up with a slippery coil.

- I like to let the shape form organically when I am working with coils, but you can refer to a drawing, photo or template as you are constructing to make sure you are following a particular shape. (See this on page 170 in the Coiled Vase project.)

- If the shape of your pot is going to come inwards, you will need to smooth the surface as you are working, so that when you get to the end, you don't ruin the form by trying to fit your hand into the small opening.

- Always dry coiled pieces slowly as they are susceptible to cracking. Drape a sheet of plastic or a recycled plastic bag over the top while drying to help all of the coils homogenize and shrink at the same rate.

▼ STEP 2

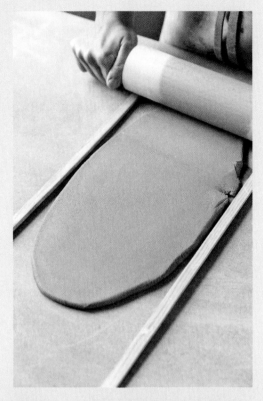

▼ STEP 3

▲ STEP 6

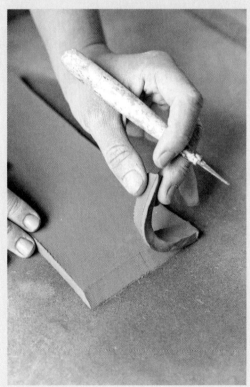

▲ STEP 9

SLAB

A very versatile method for handbuilding, slab building lends itself well to making forms that aren't round. We will start by making a cylindrical pot, however, as this is a simple way to illustrate the construction method. If you have a slab roller, you can use it here, but a rolling pin and guides are more than adequate. You can also use the provided template, found at www.hardiegrant.com/uk/quadrille/handbuilt, or make your own template for repeated cups.

Materials and tools

Clay, approx. 500g–1kg
   (1¼–2¼lb)
Rolling pin and guides
   or slab roller
Scoring tool or pin tool
Scalpel or potters knife
Wooden knife tool
Slip
Serrated metal kidney
Flat metal kidney
Sponge

ROLLING THE SLAB

1. Cut some clay from the bag, and try to keep it flat and square, rather than a cube shape. If you are using reclaimed or reused clay, make sure it is well wedged (see page 25–26).

2. Press the clay down into a flat shape using the heels of your palms. This makes rolling much easier.

3. Roll the clay out into a slab with a rolling pin and guides (see tip on guides on page 55) or a slab roller.

4. Peel the clay up and turn it over, then roll in the other direction to ensure an even thickness. I do this 3–4 times as I am rolling it out. The length of the slab needs to be at least the circumference of the cup, so if you are using a template, ensure it fits on the slab. It should be at least 15cm (6in) for a small cup – do some experimenting to see what size you would like your cup to be. The width of the slab will be the height of the cup, so ensure you have enough clay for this.

5. Once you have your slab, peel it up to make sure it isn't stuck to your work surface, and place it back down again, ready to cut.

6. On one side of the slab, using your scalpel or potters knife, cut a long rectangle approximately 15 x 7cm (6 x 2¾in) making sure the lines are parallel. Here, the height of your cup will be 7cm (2¾in), but you can amend this to whatever size you would like. Try to be efficient with the slab as we will come back to the excess, if there is any.

Turn to page 55 for instructions on joining the sides and base.

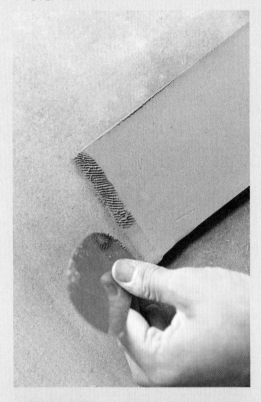

▲ STEP 13

▲ STEP 13.1

▲ STEP 13.2

▲ STEP 15

JOINING

You can either keep your join as an overlapping join and make the most of the construction marks, or you can make the join flush and invisible. To do an overlapping join, go to step 7. If you want an invisible join, go to step 9. Meet at step 12.

7. To make an overlapping join, use the pin tool or serrated metal kidney to score approximately 5mm (¼in) from the edge of one of the short sides of the slab. Flip the clay over and score 5mm (¼in) from the edge of the other end of the strip. Paint one scored side with slip.

8. Stand the clay up on its long edge, and roll each end around until the short edges meet. Gently but firmly press the scored edges together, making a cylinder.

9. To make a flush join, you need to do a mitre cut. This means that on the short edges you need to cut at a 45-degree angle. Do this for one side and score it. You can use a ruler or your guide to guide your tool in a straight line here.

10. Flip the slab over and do the same on the other edge, then paint some slip on the scored edge. If you don't flip the slab over, the joins will not meet and you will be missing a chunk of clay.

11. Stand the clay up on its long edge and roll each end around until the short edges meet. Gently but firmly press the scored edges together, making a cylinder.

12. Tidy the join up with a metal rib, wooden knife tool, your thumb or all of the above.

BASE

We now have a cylinder to mark a base on the remaining clay. Have a look at both ends of the cylinder and choose the neater end to be the rim. Place the cylinder, rim up, on the base and trace around it using a pin tool or wooden knife tool.

13. Take the cylinder off the base slab and cut out the base with the scalpel or potters knife. Score both sides and slip the base, then attach the cylinder to the base.

14. Gently tap it down a couple of times to make sure it has adhered well. Get a wooden knife tool and trace the inside of the join to tidy it up.

15. With the back of your thumb, bring any excess clay up from the base into the wall of the pot to bond the join well.

16. Tidy the whole pot up with a lightly dampened sponge, ensuring that you are not adding too much water to the clay but just tidying the surface up.

Tips

*   The guides should be on either side of your clay, and the rolling pin should be rolling on top of the clay until it hits the guides. Don't roll without the guides, as they help to prevent the clay from being rolled too thin or to an uneven thickness, leading to a weak pot.

*   It is a good idea to place a tea towel or cloth under the clay when you are rolling it out, as the pressure of pushing the clay onto the surface can sometimes make it stick.

*   Carefully pick the clay up and flip it over every now and again to ensure even rolling of your slab. This also helps to make sure it isn't sticking.

*   If you think the rim of your cup is too thick, you can trim it down with a knife. Do this slowly and tidy it up with a sponge afterwards.

HANDLES

There are many different ways to make cup handles. The following are the most common ones for handbuilding, although you may also want to look into pulled and extruded handles.

Handle sizes are completely dependent on the size of the piece you are working on, and the function that it serves. If you have a big coffee pot, for example, your handle needs to be sturdy enough to hold the weight of not only the pot, but the liquid inside the pot. If you are making a handle for a tiny teacup, a dainty handle would suit.

On the flip side – there are also fully decorative handles, like that on the side of a large vase, for example. They don't really serve a function, per se, apart from looking good, so the design of handles in this context can reflect that.

COIL HANDLES

1. Roll a long coil, about the width of a finger. The size of the coil, like the slab handle, will depend on the size of the cup you are working on. If you wish, you can very gently flatten the coil with a rolling pin.

2. Hold the coil up to the side of the cup to decide on the shape of handle and how you would like it to sit then trim the handle to size.

SLAB HANDLES

1. Roll a small slab of clay out to around 5mm (¼in) thickness.

2. Using a ruler, cut a long |strip of clay, approximately 1cm (½in) wide and 10cm (4in) long.

3. Gently bend the clay into a handle shape and hold it up to the side of your cup to decide on the profile that you are looking for. Trim the handle down to size – it may end up much smaller than 10cm (4in) long, or it may need to be longer if you have a big cup or pot. Adjust your measurements to suit the piece you're working on.

4. Use the rest of the slab to cut out handles to this size and gently bend them into shape.

5. Follow steps 3–10 on pages 56–59 for instructions on how to attach a handle to your cup.

SHAPING HANDLES

It is important to shape the handle before it is attached, as fiddling around with it too much afterwards can lead to weak or cracked joins. You might like the traditional half-heart shape, or you may prefer to give your handles a more contemporary look. I use the curve of my rolling pin or a round dowel to shape my handles, and I leave them to harden up to the soft side of leather hard before attaching them, to keep that perfect round shape. Be sure to keep an eye on your handles, though, as they will dry a lot quicker than the rest of the cup.

Coil handles

▼ Shaping handles

▲ STEP 7

▲ STEP 8

Slab handles

▼ STEP 2

▼ STEP 3

▲ STEP 5

▲ STEP 6

ATTACHING HANDLES

Handles are attached in the same way as everything is in ceramics: score and slip.

1. Decide on the final shape and placement of your handle. Hold it up to the side of the cup. With your needle tool, mark where the top and bottom of your handle will sit on the cup.

2. Trim your handle so that the top and tail will sit flush on the cup, then score both of these surfaces.

3. Score the cup on the two spots that you have already marked in step 1.

4. Apply a generous blob of slip to the top and tail of the handle.

5. Firmly press the handle onto the side of the cup, supporting the inside of the cup with your other hand to prevent cracking or warping.

6. Using your fingers or the back of the wooden knife tool, gently blend the clay from the handle into the side of the cup. Tidy up the joins with a very lightly dampened sponge.

7. Dry very slowly, with a piece of plastic draped over the top of the cups to help the joins homogenize. This will ensure that the handles and cups will dry at the same rate.

8. Be sure to not pick the cup up by the handle until it has been fired or it will snap off.

PLASTER
AND MOULDS

Plaster is a very versatile material in a pottery studio. The main property of plaster is that it is a dust and, when water is added it becomes fully solid and very porous. For this reason, it is an amazing medium to work with to create intricate moulds or simple shapes that can be used in many ways in the studio. Plaster also wicks moisture out of clay, helping it to dry out and stiffen. It can be used in a few different ways, but the main ones are to make moulds and plaster bats (used to dry out reclaimed clay).

A few notes on using plaster

- It is very important to never put plaster in the kiln as it is a very different material to clay and will explode when heated to high temperatures. Occasionally, little bits of plaster can chip off the sides of bats or moulds and it is vital to remove these from the clay to ensure that they won't damage your work.

- If you are using clay to help you make a mould, do not use this clay for any work that you want to fire. Keep it to one side, clearly marked as mould-making clay, so it is not mixed up.

- Plaster dust, like clay dust, is harmful if inhaled. When using plaster, ensure the studio is well ventilated or work outside. Always use a high-quality dust mask or respirator that is rated for use with fine particles (at least FFP2+ or N95).

- There are two main types of plaster that are used in ceramics. Look for potter's plaster (sometimes called mould-maker's plaster) or plaster of Paris (often called gypsum plaster). These are fast-drying plasters that set very hard with high detail.

- NEVER pour excess plaster down the sink as it will harden and block the drains. Always leave any extra in the mixing bucket to harden, then dispose of it in the rubbish. The same goes for any excess plaster on your hands or tools after mixing – remove any extra plaster from your hands and wipe off as much as you can with newspaper. Only then should you wash your hands.

- I have special buckets and tools set aside in my studio for plaster work, so that no plaster ever contaminates my clay or glaze buckets or tools.

PLASTER BATS

A plaster bat or slab is essential in a pottery studio. If you are working in a shared or community studio, there will probably be plaster bats available for you to use. However, if you are not in a shared space, or if you need a new plaster bat, they are very easy to make.

MOULDS

Moulds are an incredible tool for handbuilders. They help with making consistent or intricate shapes quickly and can be made pretty easily. The most common moulds in a studio are usually made from plaster, wood or bisque-fired clay. At a pinch, a mould can be made from balled-up paper or by lining a found shape with newspaper or cling film to help form the clay.

HUMP MOULDS AND SLUMP MOULDS

A hump mould (also known as a drape mould) is a convex shape that is usually made by pouring plaster into a bowl. Clay is then draped over the hump (hence the names) for it to take on that shape. Many hump moulds that can be purchased from pottery suppliers are made from wood, but they are relatively easy to make in the studio.

Make sure that when you are using a hump mould you are able to return to your project in time for it to be leather hard. If it is left for too long, the clay can shrink and crack on the mould.

As when making a plaster bat (see opposite), it is preferable to use a plastic bowl or bucket to pour the plaster into so that it is easy to release. Repeat the method for the plaster bat to make a hump mould, too. Once you have made it, leave it to dry for about a week before using it. Put your new hump mould to use by making the Slab Dinner Plates on page 104.

You can also make the opposite shape, where the bowl is concave in a block of plaster. This is called a slump mould as the clay slumps into it to form the shape.

Note

Make sure you don't leave pieces to fully dry on a mould. Because the clay shrinks as it dries, it will crack if it's left on the plaster. Remove it at the leather-hard stage and let it dry without the mould.

MAKING BATS OR MOULDS FROM PLASTER

Have a look around your studio for a container that you can pour the plaster in to, to make a bat or a mould. Ideally you want something like a plastic storage tub or box, a washing-up bowl or even a cat-litter tray – plastic is the easiest material to release plaster from. Make sure the top is wider or the same width as the base, otherwise you will not be able to remove the solid plaster from it.

Materials and tools

Newspaper
Disposable gloves if you have sensitive skin
Dust mask or respirator
Container to pour plaster in to
Soft soap or cling film – optional
Room-temperature water (never warm or hot)
Measuring jug (using millilitres)
Mixing bucket
Scales (using grams)
Plaster of Paris
Scoop

1. Set up your workspace. Find a level surface to work on; I like working on the floor to avoid any heavy lifting. Protect your floor by laying out some newspaper. Get everything you need ready now. Wear your mask from now on and make sure you are ventilating your space.

2. If you are using anything other than a shiny plastic or clay container to pour your plaster into, you may need to prepare it. If it is textured plastic, ceramic, glass or hard plaster, you can add a releasing agent such as soft soap (purchased from ceramic stores). You can also use cling film to line anything, as this will help to remove hardened plaster, but it will leave wrinkle marks on the surface of the base – this doesn't matter for a bat, apart from aesthetically.

3. Pour water into the container you are using for your bat, to just below the height you want.

4. Pour the water into a measuring jug and look on the side of the measuring jug to see how much water is needed. If there is too much water to fit in a measuring jug, pour it into a bucket and weigh it in grams.

5. Using the ratio of 70:100 for plaster to water (70g/2½oz of plaster to 100g/3½oz of water), calculate how much plaster is needed. Use the example opposite to help you if needed.

6. Add the water to the mixing bucket. Slowly sift the plaster through your fingers into the water. Once you see islands of plaster forming on the surface of the water, you have reached the approximate amount of plaster-to-water ratio.

7. Leave the plaster to soak into the water for a few minutes or until there is no more dry plaster on the surface of the water. Then mix the plaster with your hand, squeezing out any lumps with your fingers. You are looking for the consistency of pancake batter.

8. Pour the plaster into your chosen container. Give it a shake to level the plaster and tap the container a few times to get any air bubbles to rise to the surface. You can skim the surface gently with your fingers to get rid of any bubbles.

9. Let the plaster harden. After about 20 minutes you will feel some heat coming off the plaster. This means it is 'going off', or hardening.

10. After approximately an hour, flip the container over and gently tap the base to release the plaster. Leave it to dry for about a week before using the bat.

FORMULA

For a plaster bat, your ratio of plaster to water should be around 7:10:

Length x width x height = volume
  (do this calculation in centimetres)
Volume in cubic centimetres x 0.6 = grams of water
Grams of water x (100/70) = grams of plaster

Example:
For a bat that is 10 x 10 x 5cm
  (length x width x height) = 500cm³
500cm³ x 0.6 = 300g water
300g water x (100/70) = 428.57g plaster

CHEAT

My trick for doing this without calculating or measuring anything is to pour water into the container that I am making the bat in to just less than the total height I want. When making bats for recycling clay, I really don't mind what height they are, as long as they are over about 4cm (1½in). Generally, I only do this if I have a whole bag of plaster so I'm not worried about running out. I then just slowly add the plaster into the container, straight into the water, until little islands form. I mix it well with my hands, make sure I have pancake-batter consistency, then level, shake and tap it, and leave it to go off. This may not be the best advice, but if you aren't making slip-casting moulds, it doesn't matter too much if the specific porosity of the plaster differs from one bat to another.

The process of the plaster hardening is called 'going off'. You know the plaster has started to go off when it starts to feel hot and it hardens. The heat occurs from a chemical reaction between the plaster and the water.

Once is has cooled down again, you are able to remove it from the mould. It takes about an hour.

There are also loads of calculators online, but a great one is at https://plaster.glazy.org.

DECORATION

There are many ways to elevate your pieces beyond glazing them – here are a few different techniques which can add dimension and personality to your work.

TEXTURE

Texture can be very easily applied to slabs before they are made into pots, and is a great way to add interest and patterns to your pieces. There is something very satisfying about adding this depth to your creations – you can't help but to trace your fingers over the textures and think about how it was made. You can be really creative with texture – I have included some examples but the world really is your oyster here.

FOUND ITEMS

Have a look around your home or studio for interesting fabrics and textures that can be pressed into your clay. A very popular example of this is pressing lace or a doily into clay. Even tea towels or canvas often have interesting textural patterns on them. Head to page 155 for a how to use a cabbage leaf to create texture on a plate.

CARVING

Your pots can be decorated by removing clay from the surface, but ensure the piece is thick enough to remove clay without making a hole in the surface. When the pot is finished, allow it to get to leather hard. Using a loop, carving or trimming tool make a pattern on the surface. You can make little lines, or

draw full pictures with it. Carving into leather hard clay has a really wide scope and is only limited by your imagination.

APPLIQUÉ

This is a form of decoration where you add or apply a decorative, raised piece of clay to the surface of your work. Appliqués are made with stamps, sprig moulds or by making a little decoration by hand to add to the surface of your work. To make repeated patterns, stamps and sprig moulds are needed (see pages 154–155).

COLOURING CLAY

Minimalist pottery is very appealing and beautiful, but you may want to add some personality to your pieces with different colours. Because clay is fired to such high temperatures, regular paints or pencils won't survive the heat. To add colour, you must purchase specialized coloured slips, oxides, underglazes or glazes. Adding colour to your pieces can happen a number of times during the making process.

- Colour can be added to the clay itself by wedging in stains or oxides.

- Wet or leather-hard clay can be coloured with liquid clay (slip).

- Oxides can be mixed with water or painting medium, for a watercolour effect, on both greenware and bisqueware.

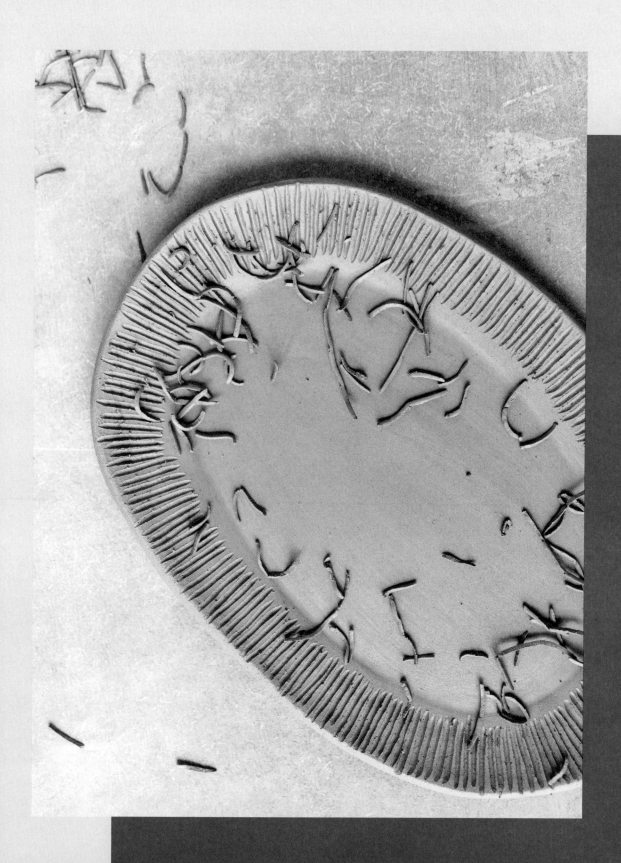

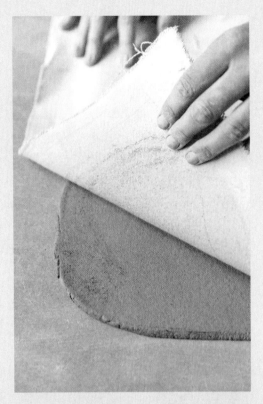

- Underglazes can be painted onto both greenware and bisqueware, under the glaze. Underglaze is a special type of paint that will survive the kiln – it contains similar ingredients to glaze, meaning it is resistant to shrinking, but it won't turn glassy like glaze does.

- Ceramic pencils, crayons and chalks. These can be purchased at ceramic supply stores.

- Coloured glaze can be applied at the bisque stage.

When purchasing colours for your pieces, ensure that they are rated for the temperature that you are firing to. The higher the temperature you are firing to, the less vibrant your colours will be – often times the colour will completely burn out or change drastically in the kiln, so do a lot of testing before committing to a final colour.

ADDING COLOUR TO THE CLAY

First, weigh the clay that you are wanting to colour. Then weigh the oxide or stain – somewhere between 0.5 and 10 per cent of the amount of clay should be added, depending on how vibrant you would like your clay to be after firing. This will need a lot of experimentation.

The colourant will usually be a powder, but it may be added to water to help mix it. Wedge it thoroughly to disperse the colourant throughout the clay.

Note

Oxides are less stable than stains and some can be toxic. Always research if you aren't sure which oxides can be harmful, and always use a good quality mask when using powders.

SLIP

The most common and cost-effective way of colouring ceramic pieces is with slip. This liquid clay is usually made up of a white base with added colourants, and ensures reasonably vibrant and even coverage. It can be used on wet or leather-hard clay, but it can't be added to bone-dry or bisque-fired clay because as it dries it will shrink at a different rate and flake off the surface. Slips can be layered up, as long as the previous layer is dry to the touch. It can then be carved into or stencils can be applied to mask out areas, to make interesting patterns or to draw pictures on the surface.

USING OXIDES AND STAINS ON GREENWARE OR BISQUEWARE

Oxides and stains can be mixed with water or painting medium to be applied to the clay. A tiny amount (1 to 10 per cent) mixed into water or medium gives great results. You can emphasize pattern or texture on bisqueware by painting into drawn lines or texture and sponging back the top surface, leaving the oxide in the lines.

USING UNDERGLAZES AND ENGLOBES ON GREENWARE AND BISQUEWARE

Underglazes and englobes are made from liquid clay and pigment – just like slips – but they also have a small amount of material that is similar to a glaze flux, which added to them to make them melt a little. This means that they shrink a lot less than slip alone and are much less likely to flake off. The benefit of this is that they can be applied to pieces that have already been bisque fired. It is possible to layer more colour onto already fired slips or straight onto the ceramic. This is a very common way of adding colour to clay.

SPECIALIZED PENCILS, CRAYONS AND CHALKS

These can be used like any regular pencils, crayons or chalk, but they are made from oxides and stains and will survive the heat of the kiln, whereas regular pencils, crayons and chalk will always fire out – meaning the colour will completely disappear – at high temperatures. If you are after some hand-drawn surfaces, these will do the trick. They are for use on bisqueware. They will often leave loose dust on the ware, so always blow this off before glazing over the top or the glaze will grip onto the dust and cause it to run. Try to do this in a well ventilated area or outside though – after you blow the dust off, you don't want to breathe it in!

GLAZING

The last way to add colour to pieces is by glazing them (see page 69).

GLAZING

When you look at finished pottery, the pieces are generally shiny or have a coating of colour on the surface. This is glaze, which is, essentially, a very thin layer of glass that sits on the surface of the ceramic.

Glaze has many functions: mainly, it helps to strengthen the ware, can make porous pieces more waterproof and helps make pieces easy to clean. If you dip your finger into some water and smear it onto the bisqueware, you will be surprised by how fast the water is absorbed. This is because the ceramic is still very porous – under a microscope it looks like a sponge. The water is wicked up by the ceramic and any excess water will be evaporated off as it dries. As well as these functional features, glaze is also a way to decorate a piece by adding colour; its finish can be shiny, matte or anywhere in between.

Glaze is applied to pieces after they have been bisque fired – that is, after having gone through the kiln once to 1,000°C (see page 84). It is dipped, poured or sprayed onto the surface of the ware – all but the base of your pieces can be glazed. They then go back into the kiln to be fired again to allow the glaze to melt.

WHAT IS GLAZE?

As a beginner potter, you don't necessarily need to know exactly what a glaze is made from. The most important things to know at this stage are what temperature your clay needs to be fired to and whether your glaze matches that temperature. This match is often referred to as 'glaze fit'.

Glaze can be purchased from all pottery supply stores in either liquid or powder form. Usually, there will be photos of what the glaze will look like, as well as information on what temperature it should be fired at and what clay it can be used on. If you purchase a liquid glaze, you can paint or spray it onto your work. It is generally more expensive to buy liquid glaze because you are paying by weight and around half of that is water. If you purchase powdered glaze, you can dip, pour or spray it on. You can also add a medium to powdered glaze so that you can paint it on, if you prefer. Powdered glaze needs to be mixed with water (see pages 74–75).

If you are a beginner potter, there is nothing wrong with using a commercial glaze. In fact, I would probably recommend it, as diving into the world of glaze is almost an entire topic by itself. In my opinion, it is better to understand how to use clay to make what you would like to make, to work out what your style is and what kind of pieces you would like to be making, before going on a long journey to understand the science of glazing.

Nevertheless, it is not a bad thing to know what a glaze is. Scientifically, glaze is made up of four main parts.

- **Glass former** – this will be in the glaze as silica. Every glaze needs silica. It is also called quartz or flint – chemically they are all the same, some are just more refined than others. Silica melts at a very high temperature, around 1,700°C (3,092°F). This is much higher than the clay that potters use can go without melting, so we need something to bring the melting point of the glass down.

- **Refractory** – or the glue that will hold the silica on the side of the pot. It is usually added to the glaze in the form of kaolin or ball clay.

- **Fluxes** – these are the parts of the glaze that brings the melting point of the glass former down so that it can actually do its job in the glaze. Every glaze will always contain at least two fluxes You can generally swap these out for each other, but they will yield slightly different results in terms of texture.

- **Colourants** – the above ingredients, in the right combination, will result in a melted clear glaze. The last part of a glaze is what brings the colour. Made from different minerals and oxides, colourants are usually added in small amounts to the glaze to achieve great results. Generally, they don't really do anything to the glaze chemically.

Knowing what is in your glazes is very important for troubleshooting if you have any problems with your glazes, or if there is a particular colour or finish that you would like to achieve on the surface of your pots which you are not getting with commercial glazes.

Glaze recipes denote percentages. When working with glaze recipes, you should use grams as your unit of measurement. You can directly copy the percentage to grams, instead of having to convert to another unit of measurement. Water is added at an approximate weight of 1:1 dry glaze: water. It is also weighed, rather than measured, when working with glaze. It is seen as an ingredient – one gram of water is equal to one millilitre. I won't convert any of these recipes to ounces or pounds because it makes the percentages of ingredients too complicated. Glazes are made using recipes and the quantities should always add up to 100%. Additional parts, such as the colourants, are not important for the science of the glaze and are added in after that 100% is reached.

Example: High fire white Glaze

40	Potash feldspar	– flux
30	Silica	– glass former
20	Whiting	– flux
10	Kaolin	– refractory
100		
+ 12	Zirconium Silicate	-colourant

This recipe makes a well balanced, high fire, white glaze. The colourant is zirconium silicate – tin oxide can also be used to make white, however it is more expensive.

If this is your first time seeing a glaze recipe, it may look incorrect. However, as stated above, because the colourant generally has no impact on the chemical make-up of the glaze, it is added on to the base formula. Water is seen as an ingredient here, too, and as stated earlier, water is used in equal ratio to the dry ingredients. You would use approximately 112ml of water.

To make 100g of glaze, you would use these ingredients as shown in the recipe above. If you wanted to make 1kg of this glaze, you need to multiply it by 10, so it would look like this: chemical make-up of the glaze, it is added on to the base formula.

400	Potash Feldspar
300	Silica
200	Whiting
100	Kaolin
1000	
+ 120	Zirconium Silicate

This recipe would use 1120g (or millilitres) of water.

Glaze, or the individual ingredients, can be purchased from all pottery supply stores.

HOW TO MAKE
GLAZE-TEST TILES

As a rule, you should always test your glazes before committing to covering a whole batch of work in an untested glaze. There are many issues that can arise when glazing. Aside from actual flaws, however, you may just not like how the glaze has turned out and you might need to amend it by adding or removing some water, or by using a different glaze altogether. For this reason, I like to always have some bisque glaze-test tiles in the studio, ready for me to do any trials.

There are a few ways to make test tiles and the easiest are shown below. You should choose whichever method works best for you and suits your work. For example, if you are making plates, you may want to know how your glaze behaves on a flat surface, so you would use the method listed below.

You should use the same clay to make your test tiles as you intend to work with – all clays fire slightly differently so the glazes may look quite different from one clay to the next.

Glaze-test tiles

1. Roll a slab of clay out, somewhere between 5mm (¼in) and 8mm (⅜in) thick. Smooth the clay with a metal or rubber rib.

2. Cut out tiles from the clay, approximately 7 x 3cm (2¾ x 1¼in) each and place them on a board to dry out. If you want to make your tiles stand up, bend them into an L shape before they dry.

3. If you would like to tidy them up, sponge the edges down once they are leather hard or dry.

4. Bisque fire.

HOW TO MAKE A GLAZE

Whether you are using a commercial glaze or mixing up your own recipe, as on page 70, you need to measure out how much you are using. As a rule, you should use a 1:1 ratio of water to glaze powder.

Safety first

When working with glaze powders, always use a good-quality, well-fitting dust mask rated for use with silica (at least FFP3, N95 or above) or a filtered respirator. Prolonged exposure to silica dust can cause an irreversible lung disease known as silicosis. Ideally work outside, or open a window, if possible, to reduce the amount of dust in the space.

SET-UP

- **Two buckets** – one with a seal-able lid, both large enough to hold the glaze powder and water (at least two times the size of the weight of powder – if you have 1kg (2¼lb) of glaze, you will need at least a 2.5-litre (4½-pint) bucket; if you have 2.5kg (5½lb) of glaze you will need at least a 5-litre (8¾-pint) bucket).

- **Jug of water, at least the same weight as the glaze** – if you are using 100g (3½oz) of glaze, have at least 100ml (3½fl oz) of water.

- **Sieve, at least 80 mesh** – this can be purchased at a pottery supply store or online.

- **Mixer** – I like to use a kitchen scrubbing brush, but a rubber spatula or a paintbrush work too

- **Scales** – I use digital kitchen scales.

- **Stick blender or drill mixer** – this is optional but makes for very easy mixing when working with large buckets.

1. Put your mask on and prep your glaze area. Then put the bucket on the scales and tare the scales.

2. Add the glaze to bucket 1 with the seal-able lid. If you are making your glaze from scratch, you will need to measure each ingredient out and add it to the bucket. If you are using a commercial powder glaze, add that to the bucket. Note the weight of the glaze.

3. Pour water all over the glaze. I like to add about 50 per cent of the total weight of glaze. Note how much water you are adding every time you pour some in.

4. Let the water sit for a minute or so before starting to mix the glaze with the brush or

spatula. If the glaze is very thick, you may need to add a bit more water at this stage.

5. Once you have mixed through all the lumps, place the sieve on top of the second bucket. Pour the glaze through the sieve and into the second bucket. You can do this in a few batches if there is too much glaze to fit into the sieve. Encourage the glaze to go through the mesh with the brush or spatula.

6. Pour a little extra water into bucket 1 to get any extra glaze off the sides and base of the bucket, and mix that up. Pour that through the sieve and into bucket 2.

7. Give the glaze in bucket 2 a quick mix, then dip your finger into the glaze. Generally, you are looking for the consistency of double cream. If it is very thick, you will need to add a little more water.

8. Pour the glaze through the sieve and back into bucket 1 again, adding any last water to bucket 2 to get rid of any glaze stuck on the sides. Then dip your finger into the glaze again and determine if it is the desired consistency.

9. You can now start glazing, or put the lid on the glaze to seal it up until you are ready to use it.

Note down how much water you used to achieve the thickness of double cream. Some glazes need 1:1 water, others need less and some need more. It is important to note how much water you have added so that you can replicate the glaze when you next mix it up or amend the amount of water to achieve the results you want.

Learn how to test fire your glazes on pages 80–84.

GLAZING TEST TILES
Glaze is applied to bisqueware – a piece of clay that has gone through the kiln once, to about 1,000°C (1,832°F) (see page 18).

Applying glaze is generally done one of three ways: dipping and pouring, brushing or spraying, and I will cover the first two on the following pages. Spray glazing is a little more complex – if your studio is equipped with a spray booth, you will likely need an induction from a teacher or technician on how to use it. It is very important to use ventilation when working with sprayed glaze.

Before using glaze, make sure you mix it well for at least three minutes. Glaze particles are heavier than water, so will sink to the bottom of the bucket. If you find that your glaze is lumpy, and the lumps aren't removed, no matter how much you have mixed the glaze, you should sieve it once or twice to remove them. Lumps of glaze can cause a flawed finish after firing. You should keep the glaze well mixed while you are using it, giving it a quick stir every 30 seconds or so (some glazes even more frequently).

1. Dip the tile into the glaze for three seconds, then remove the tile, giving it a shake to flick any drips off.

2. Once the glaze has dried to the touch, dip one corner in for another three seconds. Wipe the bottom with a sponge to ensure the base is clear of glaze.

3. Write on the bottom of the test tile with a ceramic pencil or an oxide (see below). Remember that a regular pencil will fire out in the kiln.

4. Put it into the kiln on a little cookie (see page 77), in case the glaze runs onto your kiln shelf.

How to label test tiles
It doesn't matter too much which system you use, as long as you can identify which glaze you have used on the tile. If you do a lot of glaze testing, you may end up with years' worth of test tiles and it is important to be able to work out what is on the tile if you want to replicate the glaze one day.

What is a cookie?
This is a word I use in my studio, but I think it differs in every studio you go to. It is a piece of broken kiln shelf or a pre-made coaster of stoneware clay that you can place your test tiles onto. If the glaze runs, it will run onto the cookie, rather than onto your kiln shelf. When molten glaze hardens, it turns into glass and it is very difficult to remove from kiln shelves without leaving gouge marks on the surface.

▼ STEP 2

▼ STEP 2.1

▲ STEP 4

▲ STEP 7

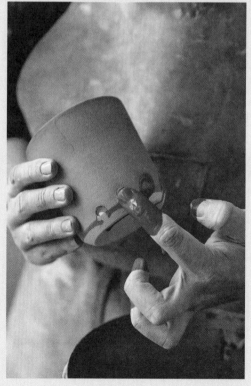

HOW TO POUR AND DIP ON A CUP

The easiest method of glazing are pouring and dipping. Most glazes that are made in the studio are for pouring and dipping.

1. Make sure your bisque-fired cup is free from dust on the inside and on the surface.

2. Mix the glaze well, then dip a measuring jug into the bucket. Pour the glaze into the cup and leave it for about three seconds. Some glazes need more or less time than this – determine this with your test tiles.

3. Pour the glaze back into the bucket. Spin the cup slightly as you do so, to ensure the glaze drips around the rim evenly. If the cup is very thin, you may need to leave it overnight to allow the excess water to evaporate from the ceramic.

4. Holding the bottom of the cup tightly, dip the cup rim down into the bucket of glaze. The rim will form an air bubble in the glaze bucket, meaning that the glaze won't be applied a second time in the interior of the cup. Dip the cup wherever you would like the glaze to go to – for example, a half-dip, two-thirds of the way up or fully submerged. Be careful to hold the cup level, as holding it on its side may cause the air bubble to escape the cup, which will make for a messy application as the air disturbs the liquid. Keep the cup submerged for the same length of time as when you poured glaze into its interior – around three seconds.

5. Remove the cup from the glaze and give it a firm shake to flick any drips off the rim. If the glaze looks better when it is thick, you may now need to dip it a second time.

6. Turn the cup up the right way again and carefully place it down. If you are using a slow-drying glaze, you may need to slide the cup carefully to the side of your workbench to avoid touching the freshly glazed surface.

▲ STEP 7.1

7. Top up any finger marks by dipping your finger in the glaze and dabbing it onto the cup. Don't smear it on, as this will remove glaze. Remove any areas of unwanted glaze with a damp sponge. Make sure you remove all of the glaze from the base of the cup.

8. When the piece is completely dry, you can carefully tidy up (called fettling) drip marks or pinholes by lightly brushing your finger over the area to make a fine dust. If you are doing heavy fettling, wear a mask and work in a ventilated area.

HOW TO BRUSH ON A GLAZE

A brush-on glaze is the same basic make-up of a dipping glaze, but a special gum medium is added to give it a texture that is suitable for brushing on. You can buy brushable glazes from clay supply stores. You will also need some brushes that are suitable for glazing – ideally, buy specific glazing brushes from a pottery store. Look for a very soft brush that is wide and thin.

The same concept of testing applies for brush-on glazes as for dipping glazes – you should get to know how your glaze looks best by putting a few tiles in the kiln before committing to a glazing style. You usually need just one coat of glaze, but sometimes two or three are needed.

1. Make sure your bisque-fired cup is free from any dust on the inside and on the surface.

2. Mix the glaze well with a stirrer then dip the brush into the glaze and make sure it is well loaded up.

3. Start to paint the glaze onto your piece. If you are working with a cup or vase, or something else that has an interior, do the inside first.

4. The water in the glaze will be wicked into the bisqueware and your brush will dry out quickly. Continually dip your brush into the glaze to make sure you are applying a full coat.

5. Allow the glaze to fully dry before applying a second coat. Pay close attention to any areas where the brush dried out and the piece is missing spots of glaze. The second coat will be easier to apply because the first layer will provide a less porous surface to glide your brush over.

6. Apply a third coat, if needed. Then remove areas of unwanted glaze with a damp sponge. Be sure that all glaze is removed from the base of the pot.

7. When the piece is fully dry, you can carefully fettle any brushmarks or pinholes by lightly brushing your finger over the area to make a fine dust. If you are doing heavy fettling, wear a mask and work in a ventilated area.

Note
When touching unfired glazed ware, make sure you have dry hands. Wet hands will pull the glaze off the surface.

To wax or not to wax?
Some potters use liquid wax to seal parts of the piece that they don't want glaze to adhere to. As glaze is water-based, the wax will repel the water and the glaze will not be able to stick to the ceramic.

Many potters apply wax to the base of all of their pieces, and some community pottery studios will require you to use wax to keep their kiln shelves free from glaze. Personally, I don't like using wax where I can avoid it. Although it saves time on sponging the bases and cleaning up drips, I find it takes the same amount of time to apply the wax in the first place. Wax also produces a lot of fumes when it is fired so if you don't have a vent system for your kilns, do not use it.

FIRING
TECHNIQUES
AND TYPES
OF KILN

FIRING

For pieces to be transformed from clay into ceramic, they have to be fired in a kiln. These are specially made to fire to very high temperatures safely – whereas home or commercial ovens aren't designed to get hot enough. There is nothing like the anticipation of opening a kiln – the huge change that clay goes through during its journey through those top temperatures is very thrilling to see.

Firing ceramics generally happens in two stages, the first of which is a bisque firing, also known as a biscuit firing (much more delicious). This is when the kiln reaches a temperature around 1,000°C (1,832°F).

The purpose of a bisque firing is to remove water from the pieces. This happens by removing all of the physical water through evaporation, but it also removes all of the chemically bound water that is found in clay. This changes the chemical composition of the clay, which becomes ceramic. Bisqueware will no longer slake down, so cannot be reclaimed. It is not watertight, so needs to be fired to a higher temperature if it is to contain liquid for a substantial length of time.

After a bisque firing, you should expect to see that your pieces have changed colour as well as having shrunk a little. The ware is very porous at this point – if you dip your finger in water and dab it onto the piece, you will notice that it is almost immediately wicked up by the thirsty ceramic. This is why we apply glaze to the piece at this point: the ceramic sucks up most of the moisture and leaves a layer of glaze powder on the surface, ready to be fired at a higher temperature.

The second stage of firing is a glaze firing, also known as a glost or second firing. This is when the pieces are put back into the kiln, usually with glaze applied, and taken to a higher temperature so the clay and glazes can reach maturity and fuse together. This can be anywhere between 1,040°C and 1,300°C (1,904°F and 2,372°F), depending on the clay body.

This is an important firing, as it will strengthen the ceramic as well as melting the glazes. The ceramic (if it is not an earthenware) should also vitrify during this firing, causing it to become watertight.

WHAT IS IN A KILN?

An electric kiln may either be a front loader, which has a door on one side, or a top loader, where the lid is on top. It will have walls made of kiln bricks, which are special refractory bricks that will not melt at the top temperatures and don't conduct much heat but insulate well. Kilns are usually insulated further with stainless steel.

Large kilns have a peephole, which allows the potter to view what is going on at any given time through the side of the kiln. Most kilns have a hole at the top, into which the potter should plug a 'bung' somewhere around 600°C (1,112°F).

The interior walls are lined with electric elements, and larger kilns can have elements on the base and top as well. Newer kilns will have a 'thermocouple', which is a sensor to measure the temperature inside the kiln; thermocouples should be checked periodically for accuracy with the use of 'cones' – these are placed in the kiln and will bend over at certain temperatures. They can be purchased from pottery supply stores and will melt at very specific temperatures. Older ones will have what is known as a 'kiln sitter' – a bar, which acts like a cone and bends at a certain temperature, is loaded into it with a little lever on top. When the bar bends and the lever drops, the kiln is the correct temperature and will turn off.

LOADING A KILN

A kiln is stacked so that layers of pottery can be loaded and fired at once. It is expensive to reach high temperatures, so it is worth firing a completely full kiln, as firing a mostly empty one is very energy inefficient.

A kiln can be loaded for a bisque firing with pieces touching each other, which means you can fit a lot more in than for a glaze firing – when glaze melts, it will stick to anything it is touching. I try to squeeze as many pieces as possible into each firing – for a bisque firing, I generally aim for double the number of pieces as for a glaze firing.

HOW TO STACK AN ELECTRIC KILN

Tools and materials

- **Kiln** – top or front loading
- **Kiln shelves** – painted with bat wash
- **Kiln props** – these come in different heights and are used to stack the shelves
- **A kiln-load's worth of dry pieces**

1. Check where the thermocouple or kiln sitter is and take care not to knock it with your shelves or pieces. On the very bottom of the kiln, place three small kiln props (three are more stable than four, which will create a wobble). Ensure they are evenly spaced around the kiln, about 1–2cm (½–¾in) away from the wall and clear of the line of the thermocouple.

2. Place the first bat on the props. This bat will usually stay here, unless it is removed for maintenance. This shelf is to create airflow around the bottom of the kiln, as well as protecting the kiln.

3. Place three more kiln props on the first shelf, in line with the props below. It is important to keep the props aligned throughout, as the structural integrity of the shelves depends on them being stable. As the kiln heats up to the highest temperatures, weak points can cause the shelves to warp or crack if they are incorrectly stacked.

A side view of
a stacked kiln.

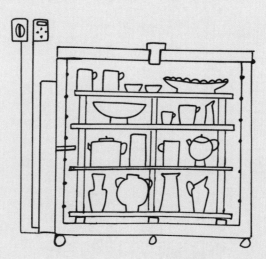

4. Place as many items around the props as you can fit into the kiln. Never allow a piece to touch the elements – make sure you leave a space of approximately 2.5cm (1in) around the elements and thermocouple for both a bisque and a glaze firing.

• For a bisque firing, smaller items can be stacked inside other pieces. Cups, bowls and plates can be stacked rim to rim. Pieces can touch, as nothing is melting. Try not to stack too many things on top of flat or wide pieces, as cracks can appear when pieces aren't able to shrink freely.

• For a glaze firing, make sure there is at least 5mm (¼in) between each glazed item so that the pieces won't stick together when the glaze melts.

5. Create another shelf by placing a bat on top of the props, ensuring that none of the pots below are touching the underside of the shelf – there should be a space of at least 5mm (¼in) between the pots and the shelf above them.

6. Repeat steps 4–6 until you reach the top of the kiln.

Tips

• Take note of the lid on a top loader, or the door of a front loader, as some kilns have bricks or insulation that can protrude into the kiln space when the lid or door is closed.

• Some glazes contain a large amount of colourants, which can give neighbouring pots a blush when particles from the pigment are transferred onto the surface of a nearby piece. Take care when loading different coloured glazes next to each other. Often these pigments can lead to cool and unexpected results, but if you want to avoid it, be aware of stacking glazed pieces next to each other.

• For the most efficient firing, when loading the kiln, try to keep items of similar heights on the same layer. For example, load cups in one layer, plates and shorter pieces in the next, and tall vases or coffee pots in the last layer. This ensures that the least amount of vertical space is wasted. It isn't always possible, but it should be the aim when stacking a kiln.

• Always let the kiln cool down to below 100°C (212°F) before opening it. This is to avoid a thermal shock to the pieces and the elements in the kiln. Your fired pieces will still be hot at this stage, however, so either wear gloves to unload the kiln or allow it to cool further until the pieces are cool enough to handle.

• Leave the kiln unvented until it reaches about 600°C (1,112°F). After that, put the bung in and/or close the peepholes. This allows any organic material to burn off and moisture to leave the kiln.

HOW TO BISQUE FIRE

Modern kilns can be programmed to a certain firing schedule. An ideal bisque firing is as follows:

60°C (140°F)/hour to 600°C (1,112°F)
100°C (212°F)/hour to 1000°C (1,832°F)
15-minute soak

The slow initial increase in temperature allows all of the moisture in the pieces to turn to steam slowly. Any faster and trapped steam can cause explosions. After 600°C (1,112°F), the water will have been removed and the program can move a little faster. The soak at the end of the program ensures that all of the pieces reach the same temperature, not just the pieces closest to the elements.

HOW TO GLAZE FIRE

Glaze firings differ hugely, depending on the clay and glaze used, as well as on what the individual potter wants from the pieces. If you want really bold, bright colours, for example, you will need to use a low firing clay and glaze.

The firing schedule for glazed ware is faster than bisque, as the clay doesn't need to release so much moisture.

A glaze firing would look something like this, but note that your own experimentations will shape what this looks like.

150°C (302°F)/hour to 900°C (1,652°F)
80°C (176°F)/hour to the desired temperature
15–30 minute soak

A NOTE ON PATIENCE

Clay is an amazing, generous material in terms of allowing you to make almost anything. However, clay is subject to physics – sometimes things may flop, slump, crack or warp. If this happens, that's OK. You can decide to embrace a wobbly pot and make that part of the character of the piece, or you can decide that it is too far gone, especially if you find a crack. If you think something is irreparable or not very charming with its unexpected warp, you can thank it for what it has taught you and put it in the reclaim bucket.

Letting go of pieces is part of learning – and definitely a part of ceramics. The clay will turn into another, better pot, filled with the lessons that you have learnt from the ones you had to say goodbye to. We live in a world of excess and I believe it is our responsibility as makers to only fire what we really love, to only put into the kiln the pieces that we are really happy with. Once a ceramic has been fired it can last for thousands of years, so it is important, when making something that will potentially outlive us, that we do it mindfully.

PROJECTS

PROJECTS

Now that we have learnt the basics of ceramics and how to make a few pieces, it's time to start getting properly creative! This chapter has a whole lot of projects for you to work through and they are structured with step-by-step instructions, kind of like recipes. This is how I do things, and I would encourage you to do it my way the first time or two that you make something, but allow yourself to learn from things that work or don't work, and come up with your own way. Same goes with design – this is my style and how I like things to look, but by all means don't let that dictate how your finished piece should look! You can use the templates provided to make your pieces in the same way as I have, or go wild and make some of your own. Once you understand the material, use this as your licence to give whatever you fancy making a go.

The chapter uses all three handbuilding techniques are covered in the Essentials chapter – pinch, coil and slab – but within the Projects, you'll find that many are combined to realise a finished piece. The projects are ordered from easiest to most complex, so there's something here for every potter.

Note on the templates

I have provided the templates for some of the projects in this book and they are available to download and print out from: www.hardiegrant.com/uk/quadrille/handbuilt. The templates are all actual size but some will require piecing together to create the desired shape. As a reminder – these templates are guides only and you can always draw these freehand if you prefer.

LITTLE WONKY DISHES

This is a quick and easy project, so you can make loads of these dishes at once. These little dishes can be used for anything around the home and they make great little gifts. You could even cut a few holes into them and add a footring to the base to make a soap dish. I use a cookie cutter for my wonky dishes so they're all uniform. I like to make them playful and add textures, have fun with surface decoration and glaze them all differently. It makes the repeated shape quite satisfying when they are all a family of pieces, but not all identical.

I use a bisque mould for this – I made a pinch pot with a flat base, which makes the perfect shape to press my dishes into. You can experiment with anything to make your little dishes from – I used to use the base of muffin tins with a small square of newspaper in-between to stop the clay from sticking.

Materials and tools

Clay, approx. 300–400g
  (10½–14oz)
Rolling pin and guides
  or slab roller
Rubber or metal kidney
Cookie cutter
Bisqued pinch pot or
  similar mould
Sponge

1. Roll out a slab of clay, 8mm (⅜in) thick. Use the rubber or metal kidney to remove any unwanted texture on the clay.

2. Press your cookie cutter into the clay and cut out a circle. Cut out as many circles as you can from the slab.

3. Peel the remaining clay from the work surface and roll it back into a ball and place aside to re-use.

4. Take one of the circles and place it onto the base of the bisque mould. Use your hand to gently coax the clay around the sides of the mould.

5. Remove the wonky dish. Sometimes the rim can look a little harsh, so I soften it by gently pinching it out.

6. Use a lightly dampened sponge to finish the dishes off before allowing them to dry.

7. Repeat this process for as many rounds as you cut out. You can wedge up any clay off-cuts to repeat this process until the clay feels too dry to wedge without cracking.

▼ STEP 2

▼ STEP 4

▲ STEP 5

▲ STEP 5.1

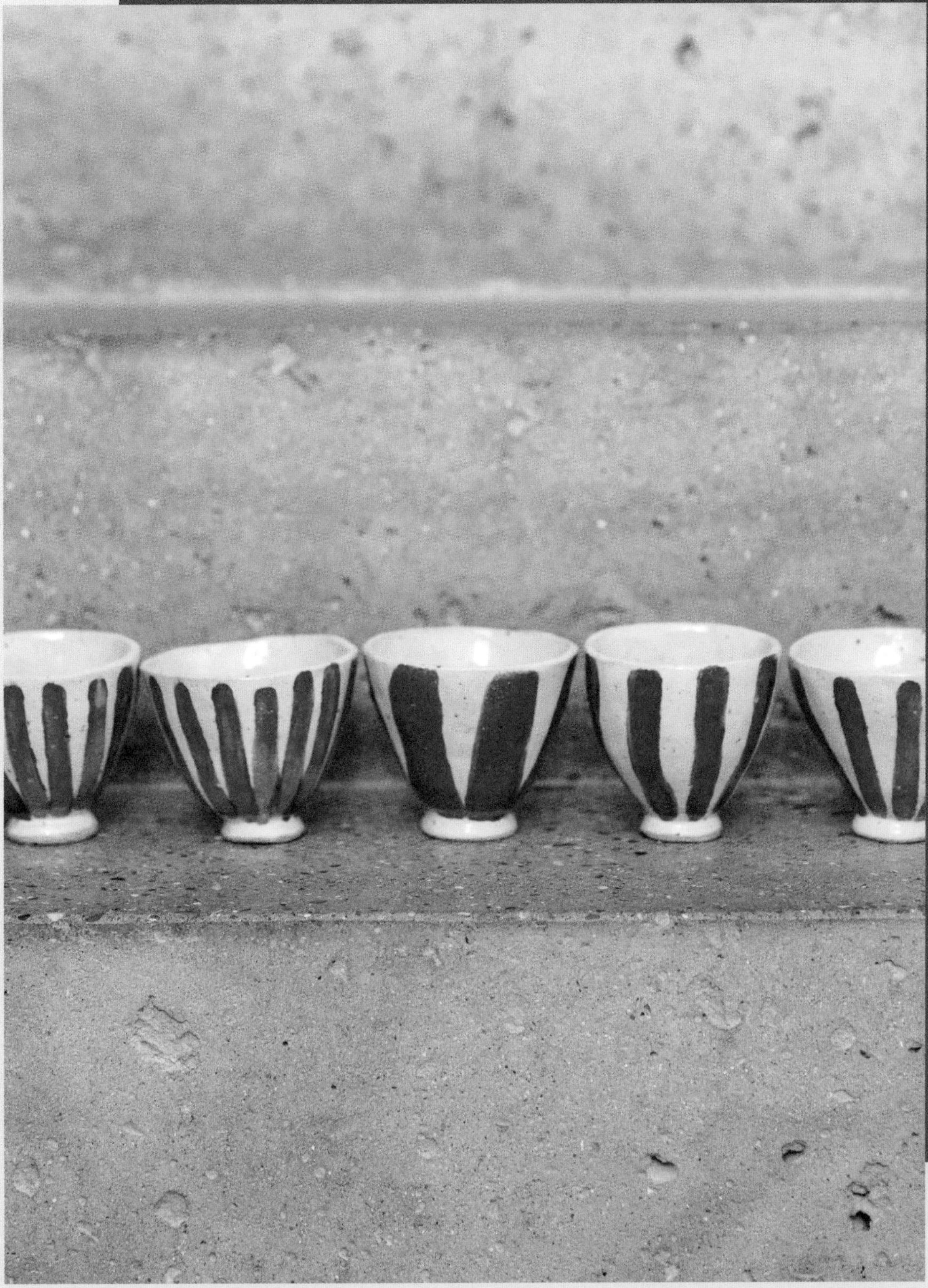

PINCH TEACUPS

Here you will use the pinch method (see pages 40–42) to make a set of teacups. As you are working, really think about how the clay feels in your hands, and consider how it would feel if you were holding a cup of tea. What sort of cup would you like? A large cup that holds all the tea you want, or a smaller cup that you can refill from the teapot a couple of times? If you would like to make a set of teacups, I suggest preparing four or six balls of clay of the same or similar sizes or weights before you start. If you aren't sure what size the balls need to be, make the first cup and amend the rest of them if you need more or less clay.

Materials and tools

Clay, a handful (approx. 250g/9oz)
Wooden knife tool
Serrated metal kidney or needle tool
Slip and paintbrush
Sponge

1. Make a pinch cup, following the instructions on pages 40–42. As you are pinching, take note of the shape that the clay is forming. If it is turning into a bowl, change the angle of your wrist so that the clay is being pinched inwards, rather than outwards.

2. Pinch your cup until the clay is evenly fine all round.

3. Make the rest of your set, covering the others in a sheet of plastic if the studio is warm and the clay is drying out. Check if they are all the same shape, and you can amend the heights by pinching lower ones a little higher, or trimming the tops off too tall ones with a needle tool. If you're having issues with some being wider than others, you can cut a V shape out of the cup, from rim to base, and then pinch the two sides together. This is helpful if you aren't able to pinch pieces narrow enough for your liking.

FOOTRING

4. If you would like to add a foot ring, take a little bit of clay and roll a small coil. Turn the cup upside down and place it on a small bat, then place the bat onto a banding wheel if you have one. Be gentle with the cup at this stage, being careful not to squish it or damage the rim.

5. Roll the coil into a doughnut shape, trim the ends and join them together with a tiny dot of slip. Place the doughnut on the base of the cup, positioning it in the middle, or as you want it.

6. Mark on the base of the cup where the doughnut is sitting, then remove and score both the cup and the coil.

7. Add a little bit of water or slip to either base or coil, and firmly press the coil onto the cup.

8. Smooth both surfaces together with a wooden knife tool or the back of your fingernail, and finish with a sponge. You can smooth the pinch pots with a metal or rubber kidney if you would like them all to be smooth, or you can leave fingerprints.

9. Repeat with the rest of the cups from your set.

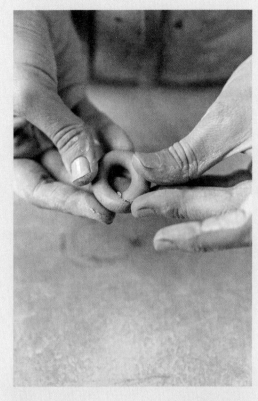

SLAB COFFEE CUPS WITH HANDLES

Cups made from slabs will result in a very different finish to cups made by pinching. Slabs can be used with templates and can make all sorts of different shapes. Slab pieces are generally more symmetrical and static shapes, compared to pinch and coiled pieces, which have more of a sense of movement to them. If you would like to make a set of these coffee cups, it will be a more efficient use of your time if you work on all the pieces simultaneously. The template for this project is available to download from: www.hardiegrant.com/uk/quadrille/handbuilt.

Materials and tools

Clay, approx. 500g–3kg
   (1¼–6½lb) depending
   on how many cups
   are required
Rolling pin and guides
   or slab roller
Scalpel or potters knife
Wooden knife tool
Needle tool
Serrated metal kidney
Metal kidney
Slip and paintbrush
Sponge

Tip

You can repurpose a take-away coffee cup as a template – carefully cut around the base and cut down the seam of the walls. I generally cut the lip off too so it's easier to flatten. A coffee cup template gives the perfect amount of taper, and it extends the life of a disposable item!

1. Refer to pages 50–55 for instructions on how to make a slab cup. If you would like a template then download and print out, in order to trace the cup shape. Alternatively, draw your own template on a piece of cardboard or thick paper.

2. Roll out a large slab or two to around 8mm (⅜in) thickness, and cut the strips of clay for the walls to the size that you would like your cups to be. Cut however many you would like in your set.

3. Roll another slab for your bases. If you are using my template, trace the base shape and cut the bases out. If you are using your own cup shape, you may already know the size that you need the base to be, but if you haven't made this size cup before, carefully roll up one of your cup slabs and hold it in place to trace around the first base. You can use this base as a template for the remaining bases. (It is worth noting the measurements in case you decide to make this size cup again.)

4. Join the walls and bases together and finish the cups, following the instructions on pages 51–55.

5. To attach a handle to each one see page 59 for instructions.

SLAB COFFEE CUPS WITH FACETING

Faceting is a great way to give interest and dimension to a round cup. It is worth putting aside a few extra slabs, or even making a couple of extra cups to practice on. There are different styles of faceting, from very fine and almost linear facets, to wider and more geometric facets. There are a few tools that you can choose to use, too. Some people use a clay wire, the same one that you cut clay from the bag with. There are tools made for faceting, but I like to use a loop tool.

Once you have played around with tools and found a look that you like, you can be more confident with the movement needed to achieve the desired finish before cutting slices of clay from your newly made cup.

Materials and tools
Cup
Clay wire, faceting tool
  or trimming loop tool
Sponge

1. Make a thicker than usual slab cup following the instructions on page 97. If you would like to make a set of cups, make all of them now before faceting. Make the cup(s) approx 1cm (½in) thick.

2. Once the clay has dried to leather hard, you can make the facets. Anchor the cup, either with your opposite hand or, if you need both hands to facet (as I do), by laying it on its side with some clay placed behind it, or you can even place it on your lap.

3. Pull the wire taut between your hands, or take your faceting or loop tool, and confidently cut a slice of clay off the surface of your cup.

4. Rotate the cup slightly and cut again. Repeat until you have faceted the whole cup.

5. Lightly sponge your cup to soften and tidy your cut marks. Make sure the join where the slab cup was constructed is still nice and strong, and reinforce it from the inside if need be.

6. If you would like to add a handle, do so now (see page 59), but be aware that the clay may be thin and delicate after cutting the facets out.

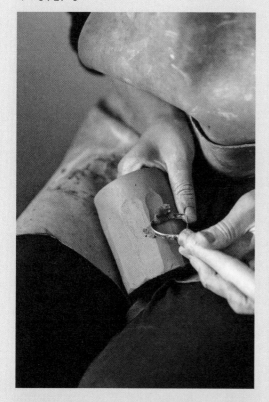

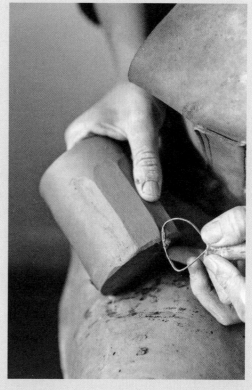

OVERLAP CUP

OVERLAPPING JOIN SLAB CUP

Another way to add interest to a slab cup is to play with the join. In the Essentials chapter, we made a slab cup with a mitred join. This is an example of how you can overlap the join, showing how it was made and allowing the join to become a design feature. Head to page 55 to learn how to do this.

▼ STEP 1

▼ STEP 2

▲ STEP 2.1

▲ STEP 5

PINCH PLATE

Much like any pinch pot, plates made by this method benefit from a lovely dappled texture from the imprint of your fingerprints. You can choose to emphasise this by making patterns with some exaggerated finger marks, or you can leave them a bit more minimal, just pinching the sides.

Materials and tools

Clay, approx 300g–1kg
  (10½oz–2¼lb) depending
  on the size you would
  like your plate
Needle tool or potters knife
Bat (as flat as possible)

1. Begin by taking a handful of clay, and squash it into a disk in your hands.

2. Using the work surface, press the heel of your palm into the clay to flatten it into a plate shape. From there, you can pinch areas that are higher to even it all out. Continue pinching until you have an even plate of clay.

3. If you are happy with the organic shape that your pinching has created, go onto step 4. If you would like a different shaped plate, cut it out now with your needle or potters knife.

4. Place the disk of clay onto a bat, and begin to gently pinch the rim upwards. Turn the bat as you work, rather than the plate, and pinch little by little.

5. If you would like to highlight the way your plate was made, press a pattern into the plate with your fingertips. Feel free to experiment with the patterns that you make.

6. Allow your plate to dry fully on the bat. Don't stack anything on it as it's drying to allow it to shrink.

SLAB DINNER PLATES

These plates are what I call pancake plates in my studio, as when they are all stacked up, they look like a stack of pancakes. They are made with a plaster mould, and this technique can be translated for any plate, platter or bowl using hump moulds. Learn how to make a hump mould on page 63.

Plates are very prone to warping and cracking, so if you are not used to making them start smaller and work up to bigger pieces. Place your finished plate on a flat surface and let them dry very slowly.

Materials and tools

Clay (I use around 1kg/2¼lb for each dinner plate)
Rolling pin and guides or slab roller
Needle tool
Rubber or metal kidney
Plaster hump mould
Banding wheel
Scalpel or potters knife
Wooden board or bat (as flat as possible)
Rasp or serrated metal kidney
Sponge

1. Roll a slab of clay out to about 8mm (⅜in) thickness, large enough to cover the mould. Use a rubber or metal kidney to smooth the clay. (Learn more about rolling slabs on page 51.)

2. Place the hump mould on the banding wheel. I like to elevate the mould slightly by placing a roll of tape, a block of wood or something that is narrower than the lip of the mould under it.

3. Gently drape the clay, smooth side down, over the mould. Using the palms of your hands, very gently coax the clay around the form of the mould, starting from the base and moving out to the rim. Do this in small sections, rotating the banding wheel slightly as you go. If you move the clay too quickly it can cause cracks, folds or creases.

4. Once the clay is in place, take your potters knife or needle tool and cut off any excess clay around the rim.

Do this by holding your needle tool or potters knife in one place, and rotating the banding wheel around the knife. Doing it this way helps to get the most even rim possible. It's okay if the rim is slightly uneven, as we can tidy it later. Equally, these plates look quite effective with a rim that's a little wobbly. Be careful to not cut into the plaster as you are doing this.

5. Set the plate aside for a couple of hours if it is warm, or overnight if it is cold. Once it's leather hard, lightly sponge the whole base and the sides of the bowl, ignoring the rim for now.

6. Run your finger around the rim and gently coax the clay to release it from the plaster mould. When it is ready to, you will feel a satisfying little pop as it pulls away from the plaster. Go around the whole rim to make sure there aren't any spots where it is still

sticking. If it is not releasing from the plaster yet, give it another hour or two before trying again.

7. Place the wooden board over the base of the plate and flip the whole thing over. With the plate now on the board, carefully remove the plaster mould. Be aware that it may have released from the rim, but the base may still be attached, so move slowly to allow gravity to help release it.

8. Tidy up any messy spots on the inside of the plate with a rubber or metal kidney, and even out any messy areas of the rim using a rasp or serrated metal kidney.

9. Smooth the rim by running the wooden knife tool over these scraped-away areas. Then blow or brush any clay trimmings off the surface of the plate and from around the rim.

10. Take a lightly dampened sponge and tidy the rim up, then sponge the inside of the plate down too. Allow it to dry slowly on a very flat surface.

Tip

This method can be adapted to any plaster mould. I have used it to make many of the pieces pictured in this book with moulds large and small. You can also purchase wooden moulds from pottery supply companies if you want to make pieces that have specific tapers or sizes.

There are many little amendments you can make to slab pieces to transform them, such as:

- You can add a footring with a coil, in the same way as for the pinch teacups on pages 94–95.

- You can make a pedestal bowl, which can be seen on pages 116–119.

- You can make different shaped pieces, such as the oval plates on pages 108–111.

NESTING OVAL TRAYS

I have a set of wooden hump moulds, which make a great set of nesting trays. If you don't have moulds like this, you can make something similar with plaster (see page 63). The purpose of this project, really, is to learn how to use a mould like this and how to get an even lip on the piece.

Materials and tools

Clay, approx 1kg (2¼lb)
Rolling pin and guides
  or slab roller
Rubber or metal kidney
Wooden or plaster
  hump moulds
Banding wheel
Potters knife or scalpel
Sponge
Flat wooden board or bat
Rasp or serrated metal kidney
Wooden knife tool

1. Roll out a slab, approx 8mm (⅜in) thick.

2. Smooth the surface of the slab with a kidney and place the hump mould onto the banding wheel with something under it, such as a roll of tape, to elevate it slightly.

3. If the slab is very much bigger than your mould, trim it down slightly with a potters knife – you do need a lot of excess, however, so leave approx. 2.5cm (1in) the whole way around.

4. Carefully peel the slab up off the work surface and place it face down onto your mould. Using wide, flat hands, coax the clay over the contours of the mould. Use a rubber kidney to smooth the clay on the walls and the base.

5. Now is the time to cut the excess clay to form the rim. It can be difficult to make sure it is even, so do this with care. Have a look at your piece and determine the point where the rim is the lowest. Take a potters knife and insert it horizontally at the lowest

point. Anchor your elbow into your body to stay steady, and use your little finger to brace your hand on the banding wheel.

6. Hold your knife tool very flat and still. With your other hand, slowly move the banding wheel around, so the clay comes to the knife, rather than the knife going to the clay. Cut around the whole piece, being careful not to move your hand up or down at any stage, especially around any bends or corners on the mould.

7. Allow the clay to harden up a little – maybe for an hour or so, or overnight if it is cold.

8. Once the clay is a little harder, take a lightly dampened sponge and tidy up the base and walls of the tray. Ignore the rim for now.

9. Run your finger around the rim and gently coax the clay to release from the plaster mould. When it is ready, you will feel a satisfying little pop as the clay pulls away from the mould. Go around the whole rim to

make sure there aren't any spots where the clay is still sticking. If it is not releasing from the mould yet, give it another hour or two before checking again.

10. Place the wooden board over the base of the tray and flip the whole thing over. With the tray now on the board, carefully remove the wooden or plaster mould. Be aware that although it may have released from the rim, but the base may still be attached, so move slowly to allow gravity to help release it.

11. Tidy up any messy spots on the inside of the tray with a rubber or metal kidney. Even out the rim by running a rasp or a serrated metal kidney over any areas that are a little higher than they should be.

12. Run the wooden knife tool or a metal over these scraped-away areas to smooth the clay and blow or brush any clay trimmings off the surface of the bowl and from around the wooden board.

13. Take a lightly dampened sponge and tidy up the rim and sponge the inside down too, then allow the tray to dry on a very flat surface.

14. Repeat the whole process to create the nesting trays if you have a set of moulds like me!

Optional
Add a couple of handles to the tray, or cut out some facets on the side for decoration (see pages 59 and 98–99).

NESTING PLATES

These nesting plates are made with a slab and a type of pinch method. I applied cobalt oxide to colour them blue, intentionally making loose and organic strokes with the brush. I like the texture that oxides can create as the pigment catches on the slightly rough surface.

Materials and tools

Clay, approx 2kg (4½lb)
Rolling pin and guides or
    slab roller
Metal kidney
Wooden board or bat
Serrated kidney or rasp
Potters knife or scalpel
Wooden knife tool
Ruler
Sponge

Colour

Dust mask
50ml (1.7fl oz) water
2g (0.07oz) cobalt oxide
Paintbrush
Translucent glaze

1. Roll out three slabs, approx. 8mm (⅜in) thick.

2. Smooth the surface of the slabs with a kidney.

3. Cut the first plate out with the potters knife. I like to cut the largest of the three plates out first, so that I know the others will fit inside it. Be free with the shape. Transfer the shape onto a wooden board.

4. Begin 'pinching' the sides of the plate upwards to form a rim. (Pinching is in inverted commas here because the movement isn't specifically pinching, as the goal isn't to thin the clay but, rather, to shape it into a rim.)

5. Once the rim has been formed, use your thumb to smooth any obvious pinch marks on the body of the plate.

6. Repeat this process to make the other two plates, ensuring they are both smaller than each other so they can nest. You can check these measurements with a ruler. Allow them to dry to leather hard.

7. Once the plates have dried a little, you can tidy any pinch marks that you missed the first time by smoothing the clay with a metal kidney.

8. Using the rasp or serrated metal kidney, trim the rims down.

9. Take the wooden knife tool, and run this over the top of the rims to remove any harsh rasp or kidney marks.

10. Dust off any little clay crumbs, and use a slightly dampened sponge to smooth everything down.

▼ STEP 1

▼ STEP 3

▲ STEP 4

▲ STEP 5

AFTER BISQUE FIRING

11. Measure 50ml (1.7fl oz) of water into a jar.

12. Put on your dust mask and weigh cobalt oxide in a little dish.

13. Add the cobalt oxide to the jar of water and mix it with a clean paintbrush. It will seem like it's very watery, but the cobalt oxide is a very strong colourant.

14. Paint the oxide onto the bisqueware. Let it pool in some areas, and build up the oxide until you are happy with the finished look.

15. Glaze it with a translucent glaze (see note below).

16. Repeat for the remaining plates, and then put them back in the kiln to be fired. Prepare yourself to be surprised at how different the cobalt looks after firing.

Note

The cobalt oxide may contaminate the glaze bucket. This is not usually very noticeable but on super-white clay, such as porcelain, it might be. If you work in a shared studio, it may be worth decanting a little bit of glaze into a separate bucket so that you don't contaminate a whole glaze bucket with cobalt oxide and risk other people's work ending up with a tint of blue.

PEDESTAL SLAB BOWL

We'll be using a hump mould for this project. You can learn how to make a plaster hump mould on page 63, or you can use the underside of a bowl that you like the curve of with some cling film over top. Using a mould means that you can make a set of these, all the same size and shape.

The pedestal on my bowl measured roughly 20 x 5cm (8 x 2in), and you can download and print the template for this project at www.hardiegrant.com/uk/quadrille/handbuilt. The short end represents the height of the pedestal, and you can make this larger if you want it to be a tall bowl.

Materials and tools

Clay, approx 1.2kg (2⅗lb)
   (more or less depending
   on the size of your mould)
Rolling pin and guides
   or slab roller
Metal or rubber kidney
Hump mould
Banding wheel
Knife or needle tool
Sponge
Flat wooden bat
Rasp or serrated
   metal kidney
Wooden knife tool
Slip and paintbrush

1. Make a slab bowl using the hump mould method. To learn how to do this, head to Slab Dinner Plates on pages 104–107.

2. Set it aside, for up to a couple of hours to dry and stiffen up a little. Whilst you're waiting, you can work on the pedestal.

3. To make the pedestal, roll out a long slab, and cut a curved strip. You can download the template provided, or make you own – it should be proportionate to the size of your bowl.

4. Cut the short ends with a mitre cut (learn how to do this on page 55), and score both sides. Apply slip to one side, and gently bring the scored ends together to join them. Tidy the join up with a wooden knife tool.

5. Place the pedestal over the base of the bowl and mark where you would like it to sit.

6. Score this place both on the bowl and on the underside of the pedestal. Generously apply slip to the pedestal.

7. Place the pedestal onto the base of the bowl and firmly press down, ensuring you do this evenly.

8. Tidy the join with a wooden knife tool and a sponge.

9. Lightly sponge the whole base and the sides of the bowl, ignoring the rim for now.

10. Once the clay is leather hard, it is more robust. Now you can trim off any areas which are uneven, or tidy any marks that were made when attaching the pedestal.

▼ STEP 4

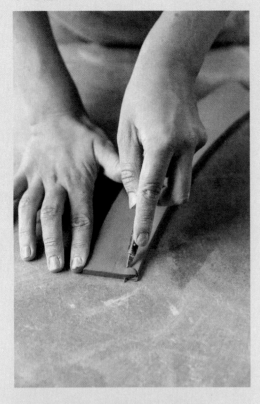

▼ STEP 4.1

▲ STEP 6

▲ STEP 6.1

11. Once the piece is leather hard, you can remove it from the mould. Place a bat on the base of the pedestal, and flip the whole piece over. Make sure the mould is released, and remove it.

12. Tidy the rim with a rasp or serrated metal kidney, and tidy by running the wooden knife tool over these scraped-away areas.

13. Blow or brush any clay trimmings off the surface of the bowl and from around the rim. Take a lightly dampened sponge and tidy the rim up, then sponge the inside of the bowl down too.

14. Allow it to dry on a very flat surface.

▲ STEP 7

CARVED PLATTER

Much like the faceted cups on page 98, this way of adorning a piece is very simple but effective. Have a little play with different tools to work out which one you like the best, but I use the corner of a small loop tool to achieve these lines. Wider facets in a platter can be an attractive addition too.

Materials and tools
Slab platter or plate (see pages 104–107
    for instructions on how to make
    the Slab Dinner Plates)
Banding wheel and/or
    wooden bat
Loop tool, clay wire or faceting tool
Dry brush
Sponge

1. Make a platter (using a mould) or slab plate (see page 104). It is worth making it slightly thicker than usual – around 9–10mm (³⁄₈–½in).

2. Once it is leather hard, take a loop tool and begin carving the length of the rim. You can use a banding wheel here, if you have one.

3. Repeat this process around the entire rim.

4. Use a dry brush to remove the pieces you have carved off the surface of the platter, or blow away.

5. Use a lightly dampened sponge to soften the carved areas and to tidy it all up.

SLAB COFFEE POT

This pot uses the slab method, and can be amended to whatever size you would like – I have made a tall coffee pot shape using the template provided. This is quite a complex make, so be prepared to take it nice and slow and allow yourself some trial and error. This project requires templates which are available to download and print from: www.hardiegrant.com/uk/quadrille/handbuilt.

Materials and tools

Clay, approx. 2–3kg (4½–6½lb), depending on the size of the piece
Scalpel or potters knife
Rolling pin and guides or slab roller
Rubber kidney
Banding wheel
Wooden knife
Needle or scoring tool
Hole cutter, approx 5mm (¼in) diameter (optional)
Slip and paintbrush
Rasp
Sponge

1. Download and print the templates for the body and spout of the coffee pot then cut them out. Of course, feel free to amend these shapes if you would like a different finish.

2. Roll two or three large slabs approx. 5mm (¼in) thick. Ensure that at least one of the slabs is large enough to fit the main body template. Smooth the clay with a rubber kidney before setting it aside.

3. Lay the templates over the clay and cut the pieces out using a scalpel or potters knife. Leave some extra clay for the base and lid of the coffee pot. These will be made by tracing around the shape of the body.

4. It is worth making a handle at this stage, too. I have not included a template for this, as there are many different shapes of handle. You may choose to make a wide strip handle from a slab, or roll a thick coil (see pages 56–59). Whatever you decide to do, make this now and

form it to the approximate shape that you would like it to be. Set it aside to firm up while you make the rest of the coffee pot.

MAKING THE BODY OF THE COFFEE POT

5. Take the cut slab for the main body and gently roll it into a tapered cylinder shape. Decide on the join that you would like – either an invisible flush join or an overlapping join (see pages 51–55). Use the score-and-slip method to join the two sides (see page 43).

6. Tidy the join up with your fingers, a potters knife or a sponge.

7. Gently place the cylinder, wide side down, onto the wider of the two circle slabs you have cut out. This is the base piece. Check the size is correct – you may need to trim the base down slightly to ensure it is flush with the circumference of the bottom of the body.

8. Score the base piece and the bottom of the cylinder. Generously apply slip to the bottom edge of the cylinder and place the base firmly onto the cylinder. Use a wooden knife to trace around the join to remove any excess slip. You may need to wait for the clay to firm up slightly at this point, as picking the pot up and fussing with the base may cause warping.

MAKING THE LID

9. While the body is firming up, you can make the lid. Place your coffee pot narrow side down onto the slab. Trace around it, then cut it out.

10. Roll a thick coil of clay, or cut out a strip from the excess slab, and form it into a ring. This will become the flange of the lid. It needs to be slightly smaller than the inner circumference of the top of the coffee pot so that the lid will fit into the pot. Check it fits by carefully lowering it into the coffee pot opening.

11. Attach it to the base of the lid using the score-and-slip method (on page 43).

12. Check the lid fits, then tidy the join up with a wooden knife tool and a damp sponge, then set the lid aside to firm up slightly. Check the fit again and trim some clay off, if needed.

MAKING AND ATTACHING THE SPOUT

13. Take the cut-out spout shape and determine if it is still malleable — you may need to spray it with some water to soften it slightly.

14. Shape the spout and connect the two sides with the score-and-slip method (see page 43).

15. Hold the spout up to the side of the coffee pot and determine where it will sit. Ensure that it does not sit too low on the side of the body, or the coffee will spill out: the top of the spout must be level with, or higher than, the topmost part of the body.

16. Trim the side of the spout so that it sits flush to the contour of the pot. Mark where it will sit on the body with a wooden knife.

▼ STEP 8

▲ STEP 10

▲ STEP 10.1

▲ STEP 11

▼ STEP 12

▼ STEP 16

▲ STEP 16.1

▲ STEP 17

17. Using a hole cutter, if you have one, or a scalpel, cut out a hole in the middle of where the spout will sit. You can either cut a few small holes or one larger hole for the inside of the spout. Make sure you don't cut wider than the inner walls of the spout, so there is enough clay to join it to. Tidy the hole or holes up with a lightly dampened sponge. Score the area on the body where the spout will be attached, and score the base of the spout too. Apply slip to the body and firmly press the spout into position.

18. Blend the join well with a potters knife or your finger. You can add a tiny coil of clay around the join if you feel the clay is too thin.

19. Tidy the join with a lightly dampened sponge.

20. To thin the spout and help avoid a dribbly pour, dip your index finger and thumb into water, and rub them over the end of the spout, where coffee will pour from. Once it is thin enough, very gently angle the tip of the spout downwards. (Practise this movement on a spare piece of clay if you like.)

21. Treat the spout with extreme care before it is fired, as it will be very fragile as it dries.

ATTACHING THE HANDLE

22. Once the handle has firmed up enough so that you can pick it up without the shape deforming, you can attach it to the body. Decide where you would like the handle to sit on the coffee pot, and mark the spots on the body where the top and bottom of the handle will join.

23. Score and slip both ends of the handle and score the marked areas on the body, and firmly press the handle into the body.

24. Secure the joins with a tiny coil of clay around each one. A full coffee pot can be very heavy, so you need to make sure the handle is up to the job of holding it.

25. Smooth the joins with a wooden knife tool and a lightly dampened sponge.

26. Place the lid on your coffee pot and inspect the piece carefully. Decide if there is any more refining you need to do on it – be it using the rasp or kidney tools to finish the texture off, or tidying the joins.

27. Once you are happy, leave the coffee pot to dry. Ensure the lid is on and drape a plastic sheet over the coffee pot to give the whole piece a chance to dry and shrink at the same rate.

POUR-OVER COFFEE DRIPPER

A pour-over coffee dripper is a way to brew coffee by placing the ground coffee in the ceramic dripper on top of a pot or cup, and slowly pouring water over it (as the name suggests) to create a brew that will slowly drip into the vessel below. A fabric or paper filter is used to line the dripper to make sure the resulting coffee remains free from ground beans. You could use your coffee pot from page 122, or you can brew straight into a cup (see pages 94 or 97). Download and print the templates from www.hardiegrant.com/uk/quadrille/handbuilt.

Materials and tools

Clay, approx. 1kg (2¼lb)
Wooden board or bat
Rolling pin and guides
    or slab roller
Rubber kidney
Potters knife
Wooden knife tool
Scalpel
Needle tool or scoring tool
Hole cutter, approx 5mm
    (¼in) diameter (optional),
    or potters knife
Slip and paintbrush
Sponge

1. Roll out a slab of clay or two, large enough to fit the template, and two circles, wider than the lip of your favourite cup or coffee pot. Smooth the clay out with a rubber kidney. Place the template onto the clay and using a potters knife, cut this out too.

2. Cut out a circle from the slab, wide enough to fit comfortably over the rim of your favourite cup or coffee pot. If it is narrower than the cup or pot, it won't be functional. Note that the wet clay will shrink as it dries and is fired, so increase the diameter by 10–15 per cent.

3. Check the cone of the dripper by rolling the larger piece of clay up, leaving a small hole at the bottom, approx. 2–3cm (¾–1¼in). Decide if you'd like a mitre join or overlapping join (see pages 50–51). Mark where

the piece will join, trim the short edges if need be, and score.

4. Score both edges of the join, apply slip to one side, and roll the cone shape up. Press the join firmly to secure it.

5. Tidy the join with your fingers, a wooden knife tool or a lightly dampened sponge. If you are doing an invisible join, blend it well at this point.

6. Roll a coil, or cut a ring out of a slab of clay, and make it into a ring to create a foot ring for the dripper. This should be able to fit inside of the cup or jug.

7. Attach the footring to the bottom of the circle using the score-and-slip method (see page 43). Tidy the join with a wooden knife tool.

8. Mark the centre of the slab circle. Place the narrow end of the cone on top of this

and, to ensure it is right in the middle, check that you can see the centre mark on the inside. Mark the outside where the cone sits on the circle.

9. Attach the cone to the circle using the score-and-slip method (see page 43). Make sure they are firmly attached, and blend the join well to secure it.

10. Use the hole cutter or a potters knife to cut one or a few holes in the base, right in the middle of the cone.

11. You can add a handle if you would like, but it is not essential (see page 59).

12. Let the dripper dry slowly with some plastic draped over the top to ensure all of the joins homogenize.

Tips

The clay may need to harden up a bit, but it needs to be a little softer than for some projects as the cone needs to be rolled up, which won't work if the clay is too rigid; after that point, you can leave everything to firm up just a little bit so that you don't deform the shapes when you are attaching the pieces.

Ensure that none of the holes you have cut fill with glaze. Use a needle tool to remove any dry glaze from these areas before loading the piece into the kiln.

▲ STEP 7

TEA STRAINER

A tea strainer is a little sieve that can sit on top of a teacup. When loose-leaf tea is brewed in a teapot, the tea is poured into the cup through the tea strainer, which catches any tea leaves. It can also be used as an infuser to brew loose leaf tea straight into the cup. Make a note of the approximate diameter of teacup that you will be using the tea strainer for, as you need to make sure that it is not wider than the cup or too narrow to be supported by its rim. Download and print the template from www.hardiegrant.com/uk/quadrille/handbuilt.

Materials and tools

Clay, approx 300g (10½oz), depending on the size of your finished piece

Rolling pin and guides or slab roller

Metal kidney

Sponge

Scalpel or potters knife

Slip and paintbrush

Wooden knife tool

Needle tool or scoring tool

Small hole cutter or drill bit, approx 2–3mm (1/16–1/8in) diameter

1. Take a small ball of clay and pinch it into a bowl shape (see pages 40–42).

2. Ensure the pinched bowl is not too thick and not too thin, and evenly pinched all the way around. It will need to be approx 3–5mm (1/8–1/4in) thick, this needs to be a narrow bowl. You can bring the rim in a little bit by cutting a V shape into the clay, from rim to base, and blending the join together.

3. Set this aside to harden slightly, for 15–60 minutes depending on the weather.

4. Flatten a small slab of clay with either a rolling pin or by pinching it flat, ensuring it is wider than the bowl you've made, and wider than the lip of the cup you want it to sit on. This will be the lip of the strainer. Set it aside to harden slightly so that it can be attached to the bowl without it deforming or warping.

5. Take a metal kidney and refine the bowl. Ensure the rim doesn't have any cracks and tidy the bowl up with a lightly dampened sponge.

6. Using a scalpel or potters knife, cut a flower out of the slab (or any shape you fancy — simple semi circles or strips look great). Cut a hole out of the middle of your shape, the same diameter as the bowl. Ensure that the size of the bowl and the lip of the strainer (when it has been attached in step 7, below) will sit over the rim of the cup. **Note:** you need to consider the clay's shrinkage to ensure that it will fit after firing.

7. Attach the lip to the outer rim of the bowl by trimming the sides of the lip to the contour of the bowl, scoring both surfaces and applying slip to one.

8. Tidy the join with a wooden knife tool and a lightly dampened sponge.

9. Take your small hole cutter or drill bit and, from the outside going in, poke little holes in the clay. You can do this in a pattern if you would like, or just at random. These holes are most important on the base of the piece and the lower sides. **Note:** don't use too large a hole cutter as the goal of the strainer is to keep the tea leaves in; if the holes are too large, they will float out into your cup of tea.

10. Wait until the piece is bone dry before cleaning up the tiny little clay crumbs that appear on the surface of the bowl as you poke the holes through. You can dust them away with your fingers or use a metal kidney or loop tool to scrape them off, and then wipe with a lightly dampened sponge. If you attempt to clean these away with a sponge while the clay is still wet, they will fill the holes again and get stuck on the surface – there is nothing more annoying.

11. Glazing this piece is optional. If you choose to, you need to leave a surface unglazed to be able to fire it. I generally leave the bowl part unglazed, so that the little holes don't fill with glaze. You can leave the whole piece unglazed if the pot is going to fall over with a round bowl when you fire it – fire your clay to maturity, the tea shouldn't stain the ceramic.

Now that you have a tea strainer, why not make a teapot (see page 137) to use it with?

▲ STEP 9

PINCH TEAPOT

A pinch teapot can be made using two pinch bowls joined in the middle to make a sphere. As long as the join between the two bowls is strong there will be a pocket of air between them, making the teapot easy to shape. A foot ring, spout and handle can be added, and a lid can be cut out. Before starting, draw a few round teapots to help you make design decisions, such as whether you would like a foot ring, where your handle will sit, and what your spout and lid will look like.

Materials and tools

Extra clay to roll out for the handle, foot ring and spout, approx 1kg (2¼lb)
Needle tool
Serrated and metal kidney
Slip and paintbrush
Wooden knife tool
Sponge
Banding wheel
Rolling pin
Scalpel or potters knife
Rasp

MAKING THE BODY

1. Start by making two pinch bowls, as described on pages 40–42. Pinch them into the same shape and try to ensure that the rims are the same circumference.

2. Using a scoring tool, thoroughly score the rim of both bowls so that they are nice and flat.

3. Apply slip liberally to one of the scored bowls. Firmly press the two bowls together, making a hollow ball.

4. Blend the join well using your fingers or the back of a wooden knife tool. If you need a little coil to fill any gaps if the rims don't meet exactly flush, add this in as you are blending the join.

5. Once the join is well blended, you can gently shape the ball by tapping it with your fingertips. The air pocket trapped inside the ball will support the form. Move the ball around as you are tapping. Keep a note of where the join was as you are tapping – it might help to make a mark at the top of the ball before the join disappears with your fingernail or a wooden knife too. You'll be able to blend this mark in later. Smooth the ball out by using the technique shown on page 46.

ATTACHING THE FOOTRING

6. Keep the two hemispheres aligned at the top and bottom with the join running horizontally across the middle.

7. If you would not like a foot ring, gently tap the ball on a wooden surface to flatten the base.

8. If you would like a foot ring, roll a coil out and shape it into a ring that will fit the base of your teapot.

9. Score both the base of the teapot and the ring. Apply slip to the ring and firmly press it onto the base.

10. Tidy the join with a wooden knife tool and a lightly dampened sponge.

MAKING THE LID

11. Place the teapot in the centre of the banding wheel. If it needs some support, place it in a roll of tape with some tissue paper.

12. Trace with your needle tool where the lid will be cut out from.

13. Holding the teapot firmly, take your scalpel or potters knife and carefully cut out the top part of your sphere. This piece of clay will be the lid, so carefully place it aside.

14. If you can reach, take this opportunity to tidy the inside of the join where the two pinch bowls meet.

15. Tidy up the area where you have cut the lid from by smoothing it with a wooden knife tool and sponging it down.

16. Take the newly cut lid and decide how you would like it to fit. Would you like it to sit on top of the teapot, flush with the teapot or inside the teapot?

- For a lid that sits on top of the teapot: Gently pinch the lid to extend the shape outwards slightly. Place it on the body of the teapot to see how it looks and continue amending it until you are happy with the fit.

- For a lid that sits flush with teapot: Don't change the size of the teapot, just clean up the cut sides with a sponge to smooth them off.

- For a lid that sits inside the teapot: You will need to make a little 'gallery' for the lid to sit on. Roll a small coil and attach it to the inside of the teapot using the score-and-slip method (see page 43). Carefully trim the sides of the lid off so it sits on top of this gallery, or, if you would like a flat lid, roll a small slab and cut it to size.

17. Make a flange for your lid to ensure it will not fall out when you pour tea. Roll a thick coil, and flatten it out with a rolling pin or your fingers. This will be attached to the underside of your lid. First, ensure that the flange can fit inside the gallery of the teapot before attaching it using the score-and-slip method (see page 43).

18. Tidy all of these areas using a lightly dampened sponge.

19. Decide if you would like a knob for the top of your lid. If so, roll a ball of clay, and shape it as you would like. Attach it using the score-and-slip method.

20. Poke a hole in the lid with your needle tool. This will ensure that steam can be released, as well as allowing for a better flow of tea when pouring.

21. Before you start with the spout, make a handle. This can be made with a coil or a slab, depending on the look you would like (see pages 56–59). Put the handle aside to harden up a little while you attach the spout.

MAKING AND ATTACHING THE SPOUT

22. Download and print out the template from www.hardiegrant.com/uk/quadrille/handbuilt. Using the template provided, roll a small, thin slab (approx 5mm/¼in) to make a spout. There are many different types of spouts, so feel free to experiment. The most important thing is that it is sharp, to cut the flow of liquid as it pours so that it does not dribble down the side of the vessel.

23. Shape the spout and connect the two sides using the score-and-slip method.

24. Hold the spout up to the side of the body of the pot and determine where it will sit. The top of the spout must be level or higher than the topmost part of the body (if it sits too low, the tea will spill out).

25. Fettle the side of the spout so that it sits flush to the body of the pot. Mark where it will sit on the body with a wooden knife tool.

26. Using a scalpel, cut out a hole in the middle of where your spout will sit. You can cut either a few small holes or one larger hole for the inside of the spout. Ensure that you don't cut wider than the inner walls of the spout so that it has enough clay to join to. Tidy the hole or holes up with a lightly dampened sponge.

27. Score the area on the body where the spout will attach, and score the spout too. Apply slip to the body and firmly press the spout in place.

28. Blend the join well with a wooden knife tool or your finger. You can add a tiny coil of clay around the whole join if you feel the clay is too thin.

29. Tidy the join with a lightly dampened sponge.

30. To thin the spout and help prevent the teapot from dribbling, dip your index finger and thumb into water and rub them over the end of the spout where tea will pour from. Once it is thin enough, very gently angle the tip downwards. (Practise this movement on a spare piece of clay if you like.)

31. Treat the spout with extreme care before it is fired, as it will be very fragile as it dries.

ATTACHING THE HANDLE

32. Once the handle has firmed up enough so that you can pick it up without the shape deforming, you can attach it to the body. Decide where it will sit on the teapot – if it is to be above the lid, before you attach it ensure that you will be able to put the lid on and take it off with the handle in place.

33. Attach the handle using the score-and-slip method (see page 43), pressing the handle firmly into the body of the teapot.

34. Secure the joins with a tiny coil of clay around each one. A full teapot can be very heavy, so you need to make sure that the handle is up to the job of holding it.

35. Smooth the joins with a wooden knife tool and a lightly dampened sponge.

36. Have a look at your teapot and decide whether you need to do any more refining – be it using the rasp or kidney tool to finish the texture off, or tidying the joins.

37. Once you are happy, leave the teapot to dry. Ensure the lid is on the teapot and drape a plastic sheet over it to give the whole piece a chance to dry and shrink at the same rate.

Well done – a teapot is a complex make!

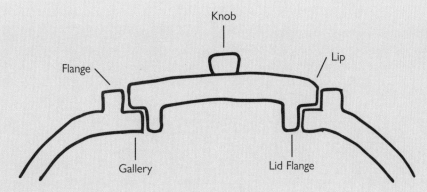

Use a flange or a gallery, or both, to keep the teapot lid in place

▼ STEP 2

▼ STEP 3

▲ STEP 5

▲ STEP 13

▼ STEP 3.1

▼ STEP 4

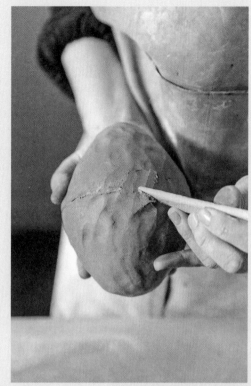

▲ STEP 17

▲ STEP 19

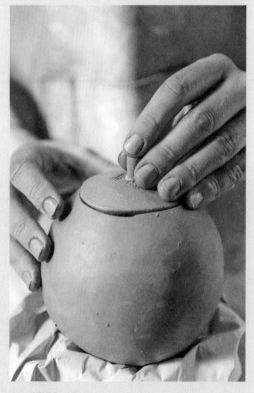

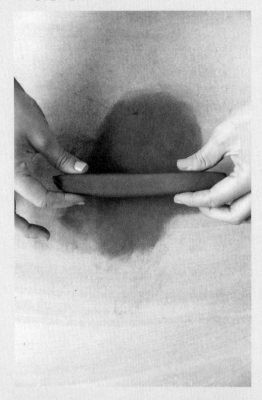

▼ STEP 2

▼ STEP 3

▲ STEP 4

▲ STEP 7

SLAB CANDLESTICK

This candlestick is a simple, minimal candlestick, which can bring a very luxe feel to a dinner party. I used terracotta clay for this project to add impact. They can also double as a bud vase, which is of course a huge bonus. It is made with a coil and slab method, but with a bit of a fun twist, and is made for smaller candles as they are less likely to topple over than a large candle.

Materials and tools

Terracotta clay, approx.
  200g (7oz)
Non-stick surface, such as MDF
Thin loop tool
Sponge
Scalpel or potters knife

1. Take a handful of terracotta clay, wedge it up (see pages 25–26) and roll it into a sausage shape. Aim for roughly 10–15cm (4–6in). Keep the coil chunky, around 3cm (1¼in).

2. Now it's time to turn the coil from a round shape into a square one. Pick it up and drop it down onto the surface. Pick it up again, turn it 90 degrees and drop it down again. Continue doing this until you have a solidly squared sausage. (Technically, this is a cuboid, but it is far funnier to call it a squared sausage.)

3. Cut the ends off so that they are square, too (rather than the odd-looking ends it currently has). Let your squared sausage cuboid dry a little, so that it is no longer floppy when it is picked up.

4. Put it up on one end, take a loop tool and start to hollow out the inside by twisting it inside and pressing down. Shake out any excess clay and continue. Be careful not to stray too far off the centre line, as you may end up carving a hole in the side of the wall.

5. Once the loop tool can go about three-quarters of the way into the cuboid, it is time to refine the top where the candle will be held. Ensure that the top 2cm (¾in), is wide enough for the candle to fit into, allowing for shrinkage (see page 149 for advice on shrinkage). I press the end of my pinky finger into the to, which helps to make it wide and round enough.

6. Tidy the inside of the little vessel with a sponge. If you have a tapered sponge on a stick, this would be the perfect tool for the job.

7. Allow the candlestick to harden to leather hard, then use a scalpel or potters knife to slice off a thin layer of clay to refine and emphasise the square shape of the candlestick.

8. Sponge the whole piece down gently and allow it to dry.

COIL CANDLESTICK

This candlestick can be as simple or as intricate as you fancy. I like to make a small collection of these in one go, so that there is a little family of candlesticks to make a cool centrepiece for dinner parties. If you decide to make a collection, start with something that will unify them, such as the same width of base or the same shape of neck, for example. You can make just one, or work on three or four at once. If you are working on multiples, have some plastic sheets to hand to cover the pieces not being worked on so they don't get too dry.

Materials and tools

A few handfuls of clay, approx. 500g (1¼lb), wrapped in the bag until use
Rolling pin
Few bats or cardboard squares
Cookie cutter (optional)
Slip and paintbrush
Banding wheel
Rubber kidney
Metal kidney
Wooden knife tool
Scalpel or potters knife
Pin or scoring tool
Dowel or long candle
Serrated metal kidney
Sponge
Ruler

1. Roll out some clay with a rolling pin, about 5mm (¼in). Cut out some circular shapes for the bases of your candlesticks. I cut a few different sizes to make the layers of my candlesticks. Each candlestick will use 1 base, and at least 1 top piece. Cut a few extras in case you would like to add layers or make multiple candles at once. If you would like uniformly round bases, use a cookie cutter. Place each base onto a bat or square of cardboard so that you can pick them up and move them without distorting the candlesticks as they grow.

2. Gently pinch the rims of the bases up so that they become very shallow bowls. Ensure the widest of the bowls have a flat base – tap them on the work surface to flatten.

TO MAKE THE COIL TUBE

3. Roll approx a handful of long coils – try to aim for 20–30cm (8–12in). Set these aside, covered with plastic so they don't dry out.

4. Using the rolling pin, slightly flatten one of your coils. Using the serrated metal kidney, score both edges of the flat coil. Apply a tiny bit of slip to one edge. Wrap your coils in a long snake around the dowel or candle. If you don't know the shrinkage of your clay, you can use the candle you're making the candlestick for to wrap your coils around, however once you remove the candlestick you will need pinch them slightly to widen them.

▼ STEP 4

▼ STEP 6

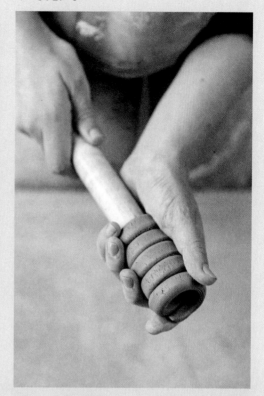

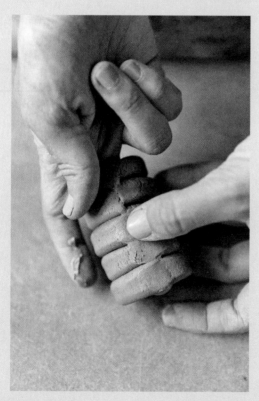

▲ STEP 6.1

▲ STEP 7

▼ STEP 10

▼ STEP 14

▲ STEP 14.1

▲ STEP 15

5. Using the scalpel or potters knife, cut through all of the coils on a 45 degree angle.

6. Gently remove the coils, and remove the short tails from each end. This will allow you to line up each coil into rings. Score both edges of the long cut, and score one edge. Press the ends together.

7. Blend the rings all together using a wooden knife tool or the back of your thumb. Make sure to pinch them wider at this stage to allow for the size of the candle if need be. If you would like your candlestick to have a few layers, make the additional coil tubes now.

8. Once you have the form you are happy with, it is time to make the hole that the candle will sit in. If you have made a clay ruler (see page 23) and know what your shrinkage rate is, you can measure your candle and add this percentage to the hole – so if the shrink rate is 10 per cent and your candle is 2cm (¾in) in diameter, make the hole 2.2cm (⅞in) in diameter. If you don't know the shrink rate of your clay, it is worth making a slightly tapered hole. If the hole is too big or too small, the candle can be melted to fit, but this makes it much more likely to topple out, which may be a fire hazard. Ensure that the hole is deep enough for the candle to fit reasonably snugly – about 2–3cm (¾–1¼in) deep.

9. Make any finishing touches to your candlestick and, when you are happy, allow it to dry very slowly by draping a sheet of plastic over the top.

TO ASSEMBLE THE CANDLE

10. Once you have your clay tube(s), you can begin assembling the candlestick. Take the tube, and place it in the centre of the widest disk – the base piece. Using a pin or wooden knife tool, mark on the candle where it sits.

11. Score around the base of the disk where the tube sat. Score the and slip one edge of the tube.

12. Firmly attach the tube to the base using slip, and blend the two pieces together with a your wooden knife tool.

13. Take a slightly smaller disk, and place the candle, dowel, or additional tube if you have made one, over the centre. Trace around it. Use a potters knife to cut out a hole out from the shape you have traced.

14. Score the base of the disk and the top of the tube. Apply slip to the top of the tube, and press the disk on to attach. Then tidy the join with a wooden knife tool and repeat steps 12–14 to add another layer.

15. Use a lightly dampened sponge to tidy the candlestick up, and allow to dry very slowly.

Tip

If you know the shrinkage rate of your clay, you can measure the candle's diameter, and add your shrinkage to it. You can determine your shrinkage rate by making a clay ruler (page 23). I have a dowel in my studio that is exactly 11 per cent wider in diameter than generic dinner candles, which is perfect for wrapping coils around and making a ideal sized candlestick. You can use a candle for this too, just make sure you pinch the coils to widen them out.

STRAWBERRY PLATTER

Using the method shown on pages 104–107 (Slab Dinner Plates), you can amend this to any shaped mould. I have used an oval platter shape for this project and made the strawberries from a sprig mould.

Highly decorative pieces like this are such a fun addition to any dinner party – the strawberry appliqué has no function apart from looking like a snack itself.

Materials and tools

Slab platter (use the same method as the Slab Dinner Plates on pages 104–107)
Plaster sprig mould (see page 153)
Clay, approx. 300 (10½oz) depending on the size of the piece
Serrated kidney
Potters knife
Wooden knife tool or needle tool
Slip and paintbrush
Sponge

1. Take a small handful of clay, enough to fill the sprig mould. Smush it into the mould, ensuring that you press hard enough to get details like the seeds of the strawberries translating onto the clay.

2. Peel away excess clay around the sides of the sprig mould.

3. When the cast is ready to be removed, it will begin to pull back from the plaster easily.

4. Use the potters knife to cut away any excess clay around the cast.

5. Using the serrated metal kidney or scoring tool, score the bottom of the cast, and the area on the platter where it will be applied. Paint slip onto the back of the cast.

6. Firmly, but carefully, press the cast into the rim of the platter. Be careful not to remove too much detail from the cast when you are pressing it in but not rubbing the cast at all.

7. Clean up the outside of the cast where it has attached to the platter using your wooden knife tool or needle tool to blend the clay into the platter.

8. Use a lightly dampened sponge around the join to finish it off.

These areas are prone to cracking, so keep some plastic draped over the platter as it's drying, and keep practicing if you don't get it right to start with!

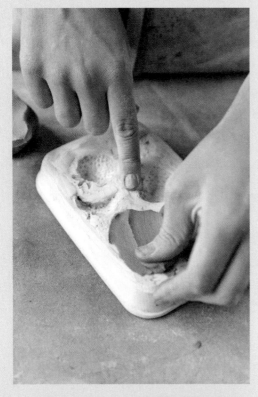

▲ STEP 5

▲ STEP 6

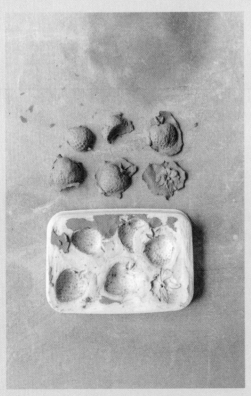

SPRIG MOULDS

A sprig mould is a fun way of making repeated detailed shapes. You can make or buy plaster sprig moulds of all sorts of shapes. Clay is pressed into the surface of the mould and a relief of the decoration is made. Sprig moulds can be made from plaster or clay, and are used to create bigger and more decorative additions to your work. Some potters use them to make handles, but most sprig moulds are used for appliqué.

LEAF PLATE

This is a cool plate that is made in a very traditional style with a slab and a leaf to celebrate the intricacies of nature. There are many different types of leaves that work well for this project, but my personal favourite is a Savoy cabbage leaf. The leaves are amazingly detailed and the texture translates very well onto clay, however any interesting leaf or texture will work for this project.

Materials and tools

Clay, approx. 400–700g (14oz–1½lb), depending on the size of your finished piece
An interesting leaf
Rolling pin and guides or slab roller
Scalpel or potters knife
Needle tool
Wide, shallow, bisque-fired bowl, lined with paper or cling film if necessary
Hump mould or towel
Wooden knife tool
Slip and paintbrush
Wooden bat
Sponge

1. Select the best looking leaf you can find.

2. Roll a slab out, approx 8mm (⅜in) thick. Make sure it is larger than your leaf.

3. Gently place your leaf on the slab and press it into the clay. Take your rolling pin and very gently roll it over the leaf to imprint the texture into the clay.

4. While the leaf is in place, take your scalpel or potters knife and carefully trace around the outline of the leaf and cut away the excess clay, then peel it away from the work surface.

5. Using a needle tool, carefully peel back part of the leaf. Once you can grab this piece of leaf, very slowly peel it off the clay to reveal the pattern underneath. Be aware that the clay can catch on the leaf and may try to come with the leaf, or the leaf may stick to the clay.

6. Get your mould ready (I used a hump mould). If you don't have a hump mould, you can place it inside a lined shallow bowl. Line your bowl with cling film, tissue or newspaper to prevent the clay from sticking.

7. Carefully place your clay leaf onto the mould and allow it to harden to leather hard.

8. If your clay leaf is in a slump mould, remove it and place it upside down on a rolled towel for support.

9. Roll three little balls of clay, the size of a large marble. Then use the flat work surface to form your clay marbles into clay cubes.

10. Score and slip the underside of the plate (see page 43) and score one side of each of the cubes. Attach these, evenly spaced, onto the base of the plate.

11. Place a bat on top of them, and peer through to check that each foot touches the bat evenly. If not, either press the bat down to squish the clay into shape a little, or remove the bat and adjust the height of the feet individually.

12. Tidy up the feet using a wooden knife tool and a lightly dampened sponge.

13. Flip the piece over and clean up the edges of the plate with a dampened sponge. Allow it to sit on its feet to dry the plate.

▲ STEP 7

COIL FRUIT BOWL

This method is fun and seems quite simple, but it requires a little bit of planning and focus. You need to use a mould for this one and, just as with the Leaf Plate on page 155, you can use a bowl covered in cling film or newspaper if you don't have a plaster mould. It is very important with this piece that you don't let it dry too much on the mould, as it is very susceptible to cracking.

Materials and tools

Clay, approx. 700g (1½lb), although you can just take it out of the bag as and when you need to use it

Rolling pin and guides or slab roller

Potters knife or scalpel

Hump mould (or a wide, shallow platter or bowl with a lining)

Pencil

Slip and paintbrush

Wooden knife tool

Wooden bat or board

Banding wheel (optional)

Sponge

Serrated kidney

1. Roll a slab of clay around 8mm (⅜in) thick. Cut a circle as a base, and place this in the centre of the hump mould.

2. Mark 6–8 points evenly around the circle. This is where the arms of the bowl will be attached. Decide if they are spaced correctly, and amend if needed. If you are partial to small fruits, such as plums, you will need to make sure there aren't any gaps large enough for them to escape through.

3. Roll or cut (see page 45) approx 10 coils. You need at least one (or two, with a join) very long coil to wrap around the whole circumference of the mould, and some smaller ones that will be the arms. I prefer a thicker coil for this project, approximately the diameter of my index finger. Set these aside, and cover the coils with plastic until you're ready to use them. If you run out of these prepared coils, you can make some more when you need them.

4. To make the arms, take a coil, and cut it into smaller pieces. My fruit bowl's arms are approx 8cm (3¾in) long.

5. Take your first arm coil and attach it to the base with the score-and-slip method (see page 43). Let the coil drape down the side, but don't trim it just yet.

6. Repeat this process for all of the coil arms.

7. Once you have attached all of the arms, trim them all to the same length. You can measure from the work surface up, or judge by eye. They can't be longer than the rim of the mould, as the rim of the bowl needs to be attached with the support of the mould.

8. Score the end of each arm.

9. Wrap the long coil around the outer circumference of the mould to create the rim, and hold it in place. Make a little mark on the rim coil where each arm meets it. Take rim coil off and score each marked area.

▼ STEP 1

▼ STEP 1.1

▲ STEP 5

▲ STEP 9

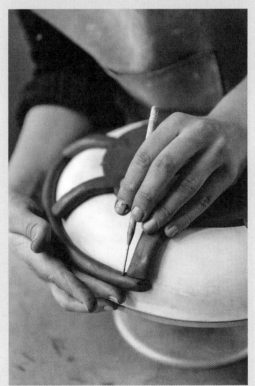

10. Apply slip to the ends of each arm, and carefully attach the rim to the ends of the arms. Press the rim coil onto each arm firmly.

11. Clean up all the joins with a wooden knife tool.

12. When the clay has firmed up just slightly, place a wooden bat or board on the base of the bowl. Flip the whole bowl over onto the wooden board and carefully remove the mould.

13. Clean up all the joins on the inside, taking care not to bump or jolt the piece.

14. As always with a coil piece, cover it with plastic and allow it to dry very slowly.

15. Once the piece is bone dry, take huge care not to pick it up by the arms or by the rim. Pick it up with two wide hands supporting as much of the piece as possible, ideally the base, as it will be very fragile until it is fired.

▲ STEP 10

SLAB VASE

Making a slab vase means you can make any shape you fancy, in 3-D. I really like making these vases. When I am feeling balanced I tend to make them as quite symmetrical pieces, but if I am in the mood for something more fun I make a completely different shape. I call these ones 'weirdos'. I draw vase shapes with a paintbrush onto a big piece of paper, and am inspired by the brush strokes. I trace these shapes I paint and turn them into templates to make into vases.

This piece is made up of three main elements – face 1, face 2 and sides – and is assembled like a pie. Face 1 acts as the base and the sides are built on top of it. Face 2 is affixed to the sides, like the top of a pie. Once the piece is firm enough to handle, it will be flipped up onto one of the sides, which becomes the base.

Materials and tools

Clay, approx. 2–3kg (4½–6½lb), depending on the size of your finished piece
Rolling pin and guides or slab roller
Rubber kidney
Paper and scissors (to make a template)
Large wooden board or bat
Banding wheel
Metal kidney
Wooden knife tool
Needle tool or scoring tool
Slip and paintbrush
Scalpel
Rasp
Sponge
Spray bottle

1. Roll three large slabs, approx the size of A3 paper (297 x 420mm/ 11¾ x 16½in) and 8–10mm (⅜–½in) thick.

2. Smooth the clay with a rubber kidney. Set the slabs aside on a flat surface to harden up a little.

MAKING THE TEMPLATE

3. Start by drawing some vase shapes on a piece of paper, either symmetrical or weirdo shapes – just let your hand go wild here. You don't need to make anything that is too over the top, but it is a great way to explore different shapes to find one you are happy with.

I have also provided a template to get you started. Visit www.hardiegrant.com/uk/quadrille/handbuilt to download the template.

4. Once you have settled on a shape, draw it on a large piece of paper, either A4 (210 x297mm/ 8¼ x 11¾in) or A3 (297 x 420mm/ 11¾ x 16½in) size. It must be smaller than the slabs you have rolled. Note that the larger you go, the more complex the build will become.

5. Cut your paper template out.

CUTTING THE CLAY

6. Place the paper template over two of the slabs of clay to check that they are both large enough for the whole template. If there is space, place the template off to one side as much as possible, as the remaining clay can be used to cut the side strips from. Try to be as efficient with the clay as possible.

7. Using the template and the scalpel or potters knife, cut two of the same shapes out of the clay. These are the two faces.

8. Decide how deep your piece should be. A good starting point is 5cm (2in).

9. Cut as many 5cm (2in) – or whatever size you decided – strips of clay from the remaining slab. Ensure these are cut as long as possible.

ASSEMBLING THE VASE

10. Once the strips have had enough time to firm up a little, around 30 minutes–2 hours depending on the weather, it's time to assemble the piece. Start by having Face 1 flat on a bat, and score where the base piece will attach.

11. Cut one of the 5cm (2in) strips to fit the base of the piece. Ensure it is very flat.

12. Score one of the edges of the strip, and apply slip over where you have scored.

13. Firmly affix the base piece to Face 1.

14. Continue to build the walls by selecting and attaching side pieces to fit the shape of Face 1. Where there is a bend or a curve, gently guide the clay into these shapes. If the clay is on the dry side, spray it with water so you can bend it without it cracking. Score the edge of each strip and apply slip to the scored edge of Face 1 as you attach each side piece, remembering to also score and slip areas where any of the side pieces join one another vertically (see page 43).

15. Using a cookie cutter, cut the neck of the vase. You can also decide to leave a gap in the side pieces to create an opening without having to cut anything out.

▼ STEP 7

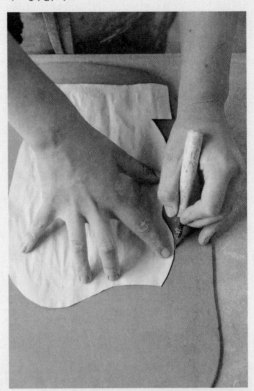

▲ STEP 14.1

▼ STEP 10

▼ STEP 14

▲ STEP 14.2

▲ STEP 14.3

▲ STEP 20.1

▲ STEP 22

16. Once all of the side pieces are attached to Face 1, and to each other, ensure that all of the joins are firmly pressed together, and clean them up with a wooden knife tool.

17. Score the top of all of the side pieces, and score Face 2 where it will join. Note that if your piece is not symmetrical, Face 2 will need to be facing the correct way, so be sure to score the underside.

18. Check the consistency of Face 2 – if you can pick it up and it doesn't warp under its own weight, you can attach it. If it does, wait a little longer so that it doesn't slump in the middle. Also check the walls – if they are too soft, they will bow under the weight of Face 2.

19. Apply slip on the scored sides, over the whole area where Face 2 will join.

20. Carefully place Face 2 onto the walls, as if it is a lid. Firmly press where the walls meet the face so that the join is secure. I use a rolling pin to very gently roll the pieces in place – it's important to not apply so much weight that the sides will bow, but enough to really have the sides and faces adhere to each other.

FINISHING THE VASE

21. Gently pick the piece up and place it on its base. You can now see the vase as it will stand when it is finished.

22. Tidy up the joins and the surfaces with a wooden knife tool or, if you need to trim excess clay, a scalpel or a potters knife. A rasp can be used when the clay is on the drier side of leather hard.

23. Once it is trimmed back, use a metal or rubber kidney to smooth the clay.

24. Finish the piece off using a lightly dampened sponge.

Notes

- The more corners your piece has, the more joins it will have. Every join is a risk of a crack forming while the piece is drying or in the kiln, so try to keep joins to a minimum the first few times you attempt this project.

- Leave this piece to dry very slowly as it is susceptible to cracking. Drape some plastic over the top of it as it dries, so that all of the joins have a chance to homogenize and no part dries faster or slower than another.

COIL VASE

Coiling is a great way to make a vase or a larger vessel as the form can be considered and amended as you work. It can take a very long time, though, so put on a great playlist, get some snacks and set aside a good few hours for this project. Coiling large pieces is meditative but requires patience, so be prepared to take it nice and slow.

I find that when I am making larger coiled pieces it really helps me to have a drawing to work to, as I can get a little lost if I am making it without a plan. I like to draw the shape I have in mind first, and then I draw another 10–15 variations of the same piece, changing the neck, handle or shoulder each time. Usually, having done this exercise, I don't end up making the first design but settle on one of the other versions.

It can also help to make a paper or cardboard stencil to hold up to your vase as you are making it. This is optional, but it does help you to keep all the proportions correct. To make a stencil, draw one half of your shape onto a piece of cardboard and cut it out. You'll be using the cut out outline of the stencil here, rather than the vase shape itself. Cut the bottom off, so that the stencil starts where your vase starts too. As you are building, the stencil will help to decide where you need to layer your next coil.

Materials and tools

Drawing and/or stencil
  to work to
Clay, approx. 1–1.5kg (2–3¼lb),
  although you can just take it
  out of the bag as and when
  you need to use it (I used
  terracotta for this project)
Rolling pin
Scalpel, potters knife
  or cookie cutter
Wooden bat
Banding wheel
Slip and paintbrush
Wooden knife tool
Sponge
Serrated metal kidney
Metal kidney
Rasp

Tip

You can start your coils off by
using a wide, round loop tool,
and cutting longways a long
block of clay. You can then peel
this out of the block and you
have a perfect, thick coil! You
can roll it out a little thinner
and longer from here.

1. Flatten a ball of clay using your palm or with a rolling pin. Then using the rolling pin, roll out a small slab for the base of your coil vase, approx 8–10mm (⅜–½in) thick. Using a scalpel or potters knife or cookie cutter, cut a circle from the clay. The larger you want your vase to be, the larger the circle you will cut out.

2. Place the base on a wooden bat, and place this in the middle of the banding wheel, if you are using one.

3. Roll a whole lot of coils, somewhere between 20 and 50 (see page 45). Try to make them consistent, approx 1–1.5cm (½–⅝in) thick, and at least 15cm (6in) long. Set them aside and cover them with plastic.

4. Score the base with the serrated metal kidney and apply a little slip.

5. Apply the first coil to the base, ensuring that it is firmly pressed down. Blend the coil down into the base on both the outside and inside. Begin coiling the wall of your piece, using a whole coil for each layer – pinch off the excess and put it aside as you may use it again later.

6. With each layer, pinch the clay just added to the coil below. As long as the clay is nice and soft, and because it's being pinched into the layer below, you don't need to score and slip each layer.

7. Frequently hold your drawing or stencil up to your vase to decide where the next coil will go – does it need to staircase out or start to come back in, or does the shape need to stay the same circumference for another layer?

8. Keep an eye on the moisture level of the clay, as you may need to spray it with water occasionally to keep it nice and soft. Don't add too much water, though, as that can make it weak.

9. Once the shape has been made, scrape the serrated metal kidney all over the piece to help the coils join into each other, and to remove any blobs of clay on the vase.

10. Now go over the rough surface with the metal kidney to smooth the clay. Learn more about this in the coil essentials on page 49.

11. If you wish to make the piece smoother still, allow the clay to dry to leather hard, then use the rasp to shave uneven areas of clay.

12. Smooth these areas back with the metal kidney.

13. Add any adornments, such as handles, to the vase (see pages 56–59).

14. Smooth it all with a lightly dampened sponge to finish.

15. Cover the piece with plastic and leave it to dry really slowly.

▼ STEP 1

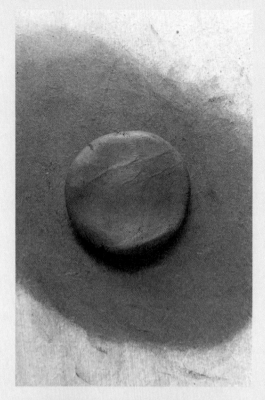

▼ STEP 1.1

▲ STEP 7

▲ STEP 7.1

▼ TIP

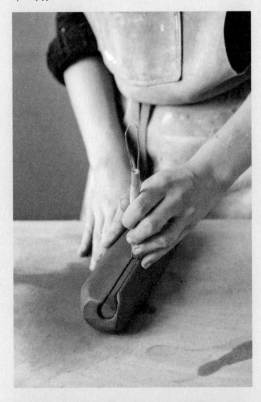

▼ STEP 3

▲ STEP 8

▲ STEP 8.1

ACKNOWLEDGEMENTS

Oh boy, writing this book has been a really good challenge. I'd like to acknowledge all of those who helped me during the past year to get here – all of the supportive comments and excitement is really appreciated.

Thank you to my family and friends who I have leaned on for support, encouragement and grammar help – I am especially grateful to my sister, Karlee.

I'm also very grateful to the team at Quadrille – to Alicia, for the huge task of putting this whole book together, and to India for seeing the beauty in banality and capturing the most amazing shots. Thanks to Charlie for completely understanding the brief even when I basically didn't give you one, and for elevating my work. And a huge thanks to Harriet for answering my nonsense, late night emails; for guiding me through the process when imposter syndrome took over; and for having me write this book in the first place. I'm sure you've read the whole thing about 50 times – hugely thankful for that.

Lastly, I want to thank my love, Jack, for his patience when my hectic writing energy has filled our flat. You're a very calm, encouraging presence and I'm very grateful for you.

ABOUT THE AUTHOR

Lilly Maetzig is the maker behind Mae Ceramics. Originally from Christchurch, New Zealand, Lilly has always had a keen interest in making. After graduating, she discovered a love for handbuilding and all things ceramics. She makes bespoke ceramic pieces for high end cafe and restaurants, design stores and online from her London studio. Lilly currently lives in London with her cat and husband.

Website: maeceramics.com
Socials: @mae.ceramics

Use the above handle for TikTok, Instagram and YouTube for inspiration and tutorials. Share your makes using the hashtag #maeceramics.

Happy making!

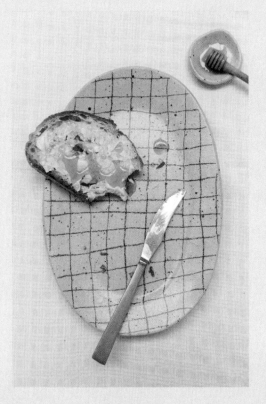

Lilly Maetzig has asserted her right to be identified as the author of this Work in accordance with the Copyright, Designs and Patents Act 1988

Published by Quadrille in 2023

www.penguin.co.uk

A CIP catalogue record for this book is available from the British Library

ISBN 978 178 713 917 6

10 9 8 7 6 5

Colour reproduction by F1

Printed in China by C&C Offset Printing Co., Ltd.

The authorised representative in the EEA is Penguin Random House Ireland, Morrison Chambers, 32 Nassau Street, Dublin D02 YH68.

Penguin Random House is committed to a sustainable future for our business, our readers and our planet. This book is made from Forest Stewardship Council® certified paper.

Managing Director Sarah Lavelle
Senior Commissioning Editor Harriet Butt
Designer Alicia House
Prop Stylist Charlie Phillips
Photographer India Hobson
Head of Production Stephen Lang
Senior Production Controller Sabeena Atchia

Quadrille, Penguin Random House UK, One Embassy Gardens, 8 Viaduct Gardens, London SW11 7BW

Quadrille Publishing Limited is part of the Penguin Random House group of companies whose addresses can be found at global.penguinrandomhouse.com